DAVID ELLIS MD, FRCSC, FACS
WITH KAREN O'REILLY

ABOUT FACE

A CONSUMER'S GUIDE TO FACIAL COSMETIC SURGERY IN CANADA

D1264947

DAVID ELLIS MD, FRCSC, FACS
WITH KAREN O'REILLY

ABOUT FACE

A CONSUMER'S GUIDE TO FACIAL COSMETIC SURGERY IN CANADA

Macmillan Canada
Toronto

Canadian Cataloguing in Publication Data

Ellis, David, date.
  About face

Includes index.
ISBN 0-7715-9158-6

1. Face – Surgery. 2. Surgery, Plastic – Popular works.
I. O'Reilly, Karen, 1952– .II. Title.

RD119.5.F33E55 1992   617.5'20592   C92-093162-6

1 2 3 4 5 J D 96 95 94 93 92

Cover and text design: Brant Cowie/ArtPlus Limited
Cover photo: André Plessel
Illustrations: Lianne Friesen
Photo p.135: Courtesy of McGhan Medical Corporation
Photo p.139: Courtesy of W.L. Gore & Associates Inc.

Macmillan Canada
A Division of Canada Publishing Corporation
Toronto, Ontario, Canada

Printed in Canada

Contents

Preface

I HAVE PRACTICED MEDICINE in the area of facial plastic and cosmetic surgery within the specialty of otolaryngology for over twenty years, and I have written this book to give readers some insight into facial cosmetic procedures. Neither my practice nor this book would have been possible without the support and encouragement of a number of people and I would like to acknowledge some of them here.

Dr. Wilfred Goodman and Dr. T. David Briant, both of Toronto, aroused my interest in the field while I was studying as a resident. In my year of fellowship training, sponsored by The American Academy of Facial Plastic & Reconstructive Surgery, Dr. William Wright of Houston, Dr. Jack Anderson of New Orleans and Dr. Richard Webster of Boston honed my skills, my knowledge and my enthusiasm in the area of facial plastic surgery.

My desire to continually upgrade my skills and knowledge in this area has allowed me to enhance the skills of my fellows. Over the years I have shared my professional knowledge with the following:

Dr. Haitham Masri of Ann Arbor, Michigan (1987-8)

Dr. Arif Shaikh of Palm Desert, California (1988-9)

Dr. Eric Gage of Sacramento, California (1989-90)

Dr. John Keohane of Edmonton, Alberta (1990-1)

Dr. Lee Kleiman of Baltimore, Maryland (1991-2)

I would like to thank Karen O'Reilly for the wisdom of her words and for making difficult medical concepts clear for the reader. During the writing of this book she worked very hard in my operating room suite, talking to patients and learning those concepts. Without her skills the information in *About Face* would be lost in a babble of medical jargon and "technotalk."

Mary Cairns, my office manager for most of my professional life, and my office staff of Vicky, Suzie, and Cindy have kept me organized and have been instrumental in keeping my office running smoothly. Many thanks to Mary and the staff!

Lastly, I would like to thank my wife, Craig; my daughter, Whitney; and my son, Trevor, who have always understood my dedication to my practice and my teaching, and who have accepted my sudden absences when I am called by the hospital. Without their steady support and trust, I would not be able to devote myself to my work. Indeed, I am lucky to have an excellent family life and a profession I enjoy.

DAVID ELLIS

Introduction
The Surgery of Happiness

M Y FATHER WAS IN THE JEWELRY BUSINESS, and when I was a young boy I spent hours with him watching cutters bent over their workbenches, searching for capillary flaws in tiny gems. Theirs was the art of cutting and polishing, of creating beauty in tiny faces of diamond and ruby and emerald. They wore jewelers' lamps strapped to their foreheads, and sometimes a magnifying loop. It was the peace and quiet of the haloed work that I liked, the focus on the beauty at hand. My father once told me that he felt a kind of responsibility toward the selection of each stone, that it was up to him to see the beauty inside and describe it to his customers.

There were no surgeons in my family, though my great-great-grandfather, whose name was Passmore May, was a pathologist in Toronto, and my father's father was a dentist. My love for beauty came from my father, but my love for medicine — what led me to become a facial cosmetic surgeon, an otolaryngologist — started with a bomb.

I was fifteen and growing up in the leafy Toronto neighborhood of Rosedale when I started to dabble in scientific experiments. With one of my friends, a boy who lived across the street, I hooked up a kind of telegraph line between our houses with the wires draped through the trees; we had a code for exchanging secret messages.

One day, with another boy who was and still is a close friend, I made a pipe bomb in the basement of our home. It went wrong, exploded and blew off his hand. His blood was everywhere.

Years later, I came across a book by an American surgeon named Richard Selzer, titled *Letters to a Young Doctor*. He wrote, "Do not be dismayed by the letting of blood, for it is blood that animates this work… Red is the color in which the interior of the body is painted." Selzer is a gifted writer, and I wished I'd had such poetry to help me through the day of the bomb. But mostly, I wished that I could have helped my friend, maybe saved his hand. I am not the first surgeon born of a desire to help, to save. My earliest work was with cancer patients, to replace lost dignity by restoring wayward parts.

It took me awhile to settle on otolaryngology (pronounced otto-lar-in-golly-gee), which is more commonly known as ear, nose and throat surgery. Or, if you like, head and neck surgery. Otolaryngology actually comes from the longer word, otorhino-laryngology, combining the Greek root words oto for ear, rhino for nose and larynx for throat.

Otolaryngologists operate within the intricate network of the ear, nose, face, sinuses, pharynx, larynx, oral cavity, neck, thyroid, salivary glands, bronchial tubes and esophagus. Some otolaryngologists incline toward a special interest in reconstructive cancer surgery of the head and neck, or they might become specialists in ear work, curing disease and infection, and even deafness in some cases. One group of otolaryngologists treats nose and sinus disorders. But because of our detailed knowledge of the head and neck, many of us become skilled in facial plastic surgery, and I knew very early that this was to be my calling.

I can trace my fascination with faces to the years I spent living with my mother and her father while my father was away at war. My grandfather, Albert Samuel May, put on puppet plays for my birthday, and he taught me how to stage the classic, late-nineteenth-century Punch and Judy show with antique hand puppets. I was a shy kid, and something about the idea of being able to transmit thoughts, and even slapstick humor, as a puppeteer, was a great release. I got to know every line on every face of the many puppets my grandfather owned; they peopled my imagination. I've since inherited my grandfather's collection and added many masks and puppets of my own. I like to read faces the way other people like to read books, and so my progression toward facial plastic surgery seemed perfectly natural.

Like every other doctor, I took two years of premed training, then four years of medical school, followed by a year of internship. Along the way, I learned general surgery, orthopedics and other things, but for me, there was always something undefinable missing. One day, I began to learn about nasal surgery, and the more I got into it, the more fascinated I became. I decided to choose the surgical specialty of otolaryngology, and went on to four years of specialty training through the Department of Otolaryngology at the University of Toronto.

Complicated constructions have always appealed to me. A few years ago, there was a popular three-dimensional puzzle toy on the market called Rubik's Cube that frustrated many people but delighted me. To solve a Rubik's Cube, you must have an architect's mind and see the three dimensions at the same time as you see their relation to one another. Nasal surgery — rhinoplasty — is exactly like this. A three-dimensional jigsaw puzzle is the only way I can describe it.

I loved otolaryngology, and during my four years of residency, I was lucky enough to study with two experienced Toronto men, Dr. Wilf S. Goodman and Dr. T. David Briant, who loved it, too. They encouraged me to travel to the United States to a couple of otolaryngology conferences, as the field of study was much more advanced there than in Canada at the time. I found that facial plastic surgery, which is a subspecialty of otolaryngology, was just coming into its own. It was the new frontier, the leading edge of otolaryngology — a challenge I couldn't refuse, it turned out. I had been married only five years, and my wife and I had a brand-new baby daughter, but we pulled up stakes, loaded everything we owned into a station wagon, and headed south in 1972 so I could study facial plastic surgery with the experts on a one-year fellowship.

I should explain that twenty years ago, when all this happened, public opinion about cosmetic surgery in Canada was a lot different than it is today. At that time, facial plastic surgery was almost exclusively devoted to the repair or reconstruction of faces that had been damaged, through cancer treatment or accident. The idea of indulging in facial plastic surgery for purely cosmetic reasons was considered suspect.

Sometimes I wonder if the simple correlation of the word "plastic" with surgery didn't have to do with people's attitudes at the time. Plastic came to mean something not natural or something fabricated during the 1960s, as in plastic chairs, or plastic people. But the true meaning of plastic, as in plastic surgery, comes from the Latin word *plasticus*, or the Greek word, *plastikos*. It means pliable, something that can be created by molding or be molded itself. Clay, for example, is plastic. So are the forces of nature, with their power to mold and shape the rock and stone of earth.

The trouble with harboring derisive ideas about plastic surgery, and its cosmetic use, was that it seriously impeded progress in the field. I used to hear stories about plastic surgeons dabbling in cosmetic surgery, in private clinics or their own homes, well removed from scrutiny or guidelines, or emergency facilities for their patients should anything have gone wrong. Bad things happened: mistakes were made. These doctors would do an operation and not tell anyone about it. Nor would they dictate any operative notes, even though it was required by law. Of course, they also refused to teach techniques to younger doctors.

One day, when I was still in resident training in Toronto and before I'd made the decision to go to the States, a patient with a very advanced cancerous tumor in his mouth came to see me. There was only one way to save his life and that was to remove part of his lower jaw, which I did, giving him what we called at the time an "Andy Gump deformity." I doubt very much we described it that way to the patient. Some time later, I was sitting in a bar near Women's College Hospital on Grenville Street, having a few drinks with some friends, other medical residents, when this brave fellow walked in and ordered a beer. He used a large syringe to squirt the beer into what was left of his mouth. I told my friends that he'd been a patient of mine just as he noticed me and waved. He came over to our table and insisted on buying us all a drink.

What struck me, hard, was the obvious discomfort of my friends. I imagine they were horrified by the man's appearance, but I couldn't help thinking that if one of them were to suffer from a similar form of advanced cancer, I'd have to do exactly the same thing to them. There was no art to it, just the cruel fact of carving a chunk out of someone's face, end of story. My patient was not reconstructed nicely enough to function well in society, and it filled me with great sadness. But in those days, it was all we knew to do. (Thankfully, reconstruction techniques have been much improved since then.) Shortly after, I left for the States to study as a fellow of the American Academy of Facial Plastic and Reconstructive Surgery.

The Academy had been formed in 1964 by the amalgamation of the American Otolaryngological Society for Plastic Surgery and the American Society of Facial Plastic Surgery. The two groups were determined to lift all aspects of facial plastic surgery, including cosmetic surgery, out of their clandestine status and into the bright light of progress and shared learning. Their unofficial motto was "Knowledge is Free." I was selected as the first fellow to spend a full year traveling to different surgeons in the U.S. for the sole purpose of additional training in facial plastic surgery.

My small family arrived in Houston first and rented a one-bedroom apartment with a large-enough closet to serve as a nursery for the baby. While there, I studied with Dr. William Wright. After that, I spent time with a surgeon named Jack Anderson in New Orleans. I was supposed to go to California, but unfortunately there was some big domestic brouhaha when the doctor's wife ran off with one of his partners, so I never did go. Finally, I spent my last three months in Boston with Dr. Richard Webster, a superb teacher of facial soft tissue techniques.

Much has changed since I trained in the U.S. in 1972, especially with regard to inter-State licensing. I doubt I'd be able to move around so freely today. The Academy's fellowship program is more formalized now, which is a good thing. A fellow has to get a licence, complete one year of apprentice training, and then show evidence of this good, solid training by passing an exam at the end of the year. The Academy experience instilled in me a respect for the value of sharing information, and I have taught countless numbers of young surgeons my craft through positions at The Toronto Hospital and Toronto Western Hospital over the past two decades.

You might think by now that I am belaboring my education as an otolaryngologist, but I'm being as explicit as I can be for some very good reasons. The first reason has a lot to do with my motivation for writing this book, and that is, I want people interested in undergoing facial cosmetic surgery to have a better understanding of what they're getting into. I spend a great deal of time talking to patients, giving them the facts about what they might undergo: the good points, the bad points and, most important, a realistic view of what they can expect to accomplish with surgery. Still, many of them, I know, nod and plunge ahead without a clear idea of what they're doing. So the first thing someone interested in facial cosmetic surgery should know is: does the surgeon have the proper training for the job that's to be done?

Choosing a Surgeon

Various types of surgeons in Canada are qualified to perform plastic surgery. Now, otolaryngologists spend a minimum of five years after internship learning anatomy, pathology (the study of any deviation from normal, healthy conditions) and cosmetic surgery in the head and neck area. Some, like myself, get further training doing one or two years of fellowship in facial plastic surgery. Plastic surgeons, on the other hand, spend five years learning the art of plastic surgery on all parts of the body, so they tend to be generalists. Some generalists' training programs involve little exposure to cosmetic or aesthetic surgery. For example, a plastic surgeon might be able to remove a bump on your nose, but an otolaryngologist is trained to remove the bump, narrow the tip and improve your ability to breathe, all at the same time. If a patient has to choose between two plastic surgeons, one of whom has pursued training in the subinterest of cosmetic surgery, and the other, who has not, it would be wise to choose the first surgeon for reconstruction of any kind.

Just as the plastic surgeon is a generalist practicing on all parts of the body and an otolaryngologist is a specialist of the head and neck, there are other surgeons qualified to do plastic surgery who are even more specialized. Ophthalmologists, for example, are eye surgeons, and often they subspecialize in ocular plastic surgery, or plastic surgery of the eye and some adjacent areas, such as the eyebrow. Dermatologists spend four or five years learning all about the skin — some of them develop expertise in performing hair transplant surgery. But before you choose a surgeon for facial cosmetic surgery of any kind, it's important to learn if your surgeon has studied and continued to upgrade skills in the relevant subspecialty of cosmetic surgery. Don't be afraid to ask. In the case of otolaryngologists, those who specialize in facial cosmetic surgery usually belong to two organizations: the American Academy of Facial Plastic and Reconstructive Surgery and the Canadian Academy of Facial Plastic and Reconstructive Surgery.

There is another reason for what I hope is a forthright explanation of my profession, and that is to encourage you to choose a facial cosmetic surgeon with whom you can comfortably communicate. I have attempted to make this book easy to understand; be sure that the surgeon you choose is equally understandable. This sounds like simple good sense, but facial cosmetic surgery is like no other surgery in that it sometimes necessitates a long-term relationship with your doctor. An appendix might be removed in an hour, but a face-lift might take a year before the scars are fully healed and mature. Happily, most surgeons get along with their patients — even for reconstructive procedures that take years to complete — but there is some interesting research available on the subject of patients who make poor candidates for facial cosmetic surgery.

Are You a Good Candidate?

Much of the current research has been done by Dr. Mary Ruth Wright, associate clinical professor of psychology at the Department of Otorhinolaryngology and Communicative Sciences at the Baylor College of Medicine, in Houston. In 1982, Dr. Wright wrote that no single method of preoperative counseling or evaluation can be used with all patients, but conversely, all patient "difficulties" develop because a surgeon fails to fulfill the expectations of the patient. By difficulties, Dr. Wright means anything ranging from tears to litigation, but essentially, she means dissatisfaction with the results of facial cosmetic surgery.

The patient might be dissatisfied because a physical complication has arisen as a result of surgery. A minor example might be hematoma, where a blood vessel has leaked and a tiny pool of blood has collected under the skin. Fortunately, physical complications as a result of facial cosmetic surgery are rare occurrences and usually correctable by the performing surgeon.

But the most common cause of dissatisfaction is a patient's unrealistic expectations in the first place. Such a patient is a poor candidate for facial cosmetic surgery. The problem is, some patients are very skillful at hiding their true expectations and motivations when they approach a facial cosmetic surgeon. Over the course of a couple of preoperative interviews, the surgeon can usually detect a poor candidate and either decline to proceed with surgery, or recommend that the patient take the time to work out personal problems first before undergoing surgery.

Dr. Wright has isolated a group of "troubled" patients with unrealistic expectations about what facial cosmetic surgery can do for them — patients who are psychologically unbalanced and should be counseled with extreme caution by facial cosmetic surgeons. She divides these patients into three broad groups: psychoneurotic, psychotic and those with a personality disorder.

I can generally recognize psychoneurotic patients by Dr. Wright's guidelines: these patients show evident worry, anxiety and a tendency to somatize. A person who somatizes converts anxiety into physical symptoms. Patients with somatization disorder usually have a long list of physical complaints for which no physical causes can be found, and they often seek out unnecessary treatments or surgery — like facial cosmetic surgery. If I sense that I am dealing with a psychoneurotic, I will give him or her the benefit of the doubt at first and schedule one or two more consultation appointments. But ultimately, what this person needs is some counseling with a psychologist or psychiatrist, and I try to direct him or her that way.

Patients with a truly psychotic disorder display peculiar, disjointed thoughts and bizarre reactions to everyday occurrences. Facial cosmetic surgeons have a particular interest in identifying the psychotically disturbed patient: Dr. Wright cites two cases where patients suffered psychotic "breaks," or breakdowns, following surgery and murdered their surgeons. The first case was detailed in the *British Medical Journal* in an anonymous editorial titled, "Hazards of Cosmetic Surgery." The second case appeared in the *Aesthetic Plastic Surgery Journal*, in a story titled "Dr. Vazquez Anon's Last Lesson." And so it was.

I should point out that both the patients who murdered their surgeons had had nose jobs; that is, they were rhinoplasty patients. In a paper titled "The Psychology of Rhinoplasty," Dr. Wright explains that authorities have observed more emotional turmoil following rhinoplasty than with any other cosmetic surgery. Rhinoplasty produces more dramatic aesthetic improvement and a higher percentage of patient satisfaction than other forms of cosmetic surgery, but it also produces the highest level of dissatisfaction in patients inclined that way.

Male patients, of which there are an increasing number (up to fifty percent of all aesthetic patients wanting a rhinoplasty), are more likely to be psychologically upset by what they perceive to be unsatisfactory nose jobs. Quite often, this dissatisfaction has to do with a deep-seated identity conflict, sexual or otherwise, as the nose ranks with the penis and breast as one of the most psychologically important body parts. The hapless facial cosmetic surgeon may end up taking the brunt of the patient's frustrations.

The third troubled group noted by Dr. Wright — patients with a personality disorder — are the most difficult to identify. These patients tend to act out, to be manipulative, to have their pleasure at the expense of others, to disregard social mores and to be lacking in emotional depth. They are the group most inclined to sue a facial cosmetic surgeon for medical malpractice, no matter what the outcome of surgery might be. Frankly, their manipulativeness makes them hard to recognize because it often takes the form of flattery — hard for many doctors to resist! If you ask such a patient what he wants done to his face, his answer might be: "You're the expert, doctor. You tell me." This should set off warning bells for more experienced facial cosmetic surgeons.

Dr. Wright has identified the most troubled groups, but they are not the only people who go looking for facial cosmetic surgery when they shouldn't. You might consider measuring your own motivation for seeking out facial cosmetic surgery against information published by the American Academy of Facial Plastic and Reconstructive Surgery. The Academy has put out a text called *The Face Book* in which four types of individuals are identified as having unnacceptable reasons for wanting facial cosmetic surgery.

First, people with ill-considered reasons for wanting surgery, such as the twenty-three-year-old man who wanted a face-lift because his coworkers were ribbing him for being too old. Second, people who seem out of touch with reality, like the obese woman in her mid-thirties who came into a surgeon's office wearing filthy clothes, a ton of makeup and with her hair dyed an unnatural color; she wanted her eyelids done in order to improve her appearance. Third, people who seek surgery at someone else's instigation, like the sullen daughter brought in for nasal surgery by her beautiful mother or the wife whose husband is pushing her into doing something she doesn't want to do. And fourth, people who have a secondary motive, such as the pathetic old man who wanted a face-lift because his family had kicked him out of the house and he thought a face-lift would make them want to take him back in.

In each of these cases, the people involved were looking for "quick fixes" to life's problems. Facial cosmetic surgery, however, is a long-term commitment (I'd never call it a solution), and only a part of what should be a well-adjusted approach to life. In my twenty years of practice, I have developed a couple of mostly intuitive tests for my potential patients, at least during the initial consultation. Basically, I try to assess whether they are listening to what I have to say, and whether we will get along.

I am wary of the patient who is too much of a perfectionist, because facial cosmetic surgery is not a precise art. Facial cosmetic surgery is merely an improvement on what already exists. If a patient with a crooked nose comes in and says, "Doctor, I want my nose straight," the first thing I have to tell him is that I can't guarantee it will be straight after surgery. But it should be straighter than when we started. Or a woman might tell me that she doesn't want any sag under her eyes. I have to point out that if I were to try to remove 100 percent of the sag under her eyes, her lower eyelids would be so tight she may develop complications of a "rounded" eye or worse. (The lower eyelid would be pulled down into an unnatural, round shape instead of its normal ovoid or almond shape.) In addition to which, it is surgically impossible to actually remove 100 percent of the sag under anyone's eyes. If I am one millimeter away from perfection, a perfectionist will complain, and we'll both be unhappy.

I don't mention my unhappiness idly, by the way. The accepted personality profile of a facial cosmetic surgeon like myself is one with an elevated need to achieve, to excel, to control, to be right and to be seen in a favorable light (again, based on Dr. Wright's research). The chances are very good that the perfection I seek in my work will far exceed the perfection that my patients desire. Nothing makes me happier than a job well done, and, in fact, facial cosmetic surgery has been called the "surgery of happiness." There is no pleasanter experience than watching a patient bloom with the self-confidence that comes when an operation is successful and well-received. Young people with smoother skin after dermabrasion for acne scars start dating, kids who lose their "flyaway" ears (ears that stick out) make new friends — I've even witnessed an seventy-year-old real estate agent walk out the door after a face-lift to sell two homes in a week, the best she'd ever done.

As well as the perfectionist, I am wary of the patient with a secondary motive, like the old man who wanted a face-lift so his family would take him back. You'd be surprised at the number of people who come into my office, calmly sit down, then burst into tears when I ask them why they want something done. Quite often, this sort of patient is six months into a separation, and some of them even have arranged to see a divorce lawyer the same day they see me. They usually are highly motivated and say something like, "Just go ahead and do it, I don't want to hear about complications." The trouble is, what's motivating them is painful, but temporary, emotional turmoil. My approach is to explain to them that we can indeed do the surgery they are asking for, but that we will not do it until their emotions have calmed. In the meantime, they might need some professional psychological counseling.

This is not to say that I automatically reject all patients who have had to suffer through a marriage breakdown. I had a patient come in one day who said he'd been divorced for a year and was anxious to get on with his life and "get out into the meet market." His choice of words was a little off-putting, but I could see that he'd gone through the worst of his emotional strife and simply thought that getting rid of the bags under his eyes might give him some self-confidence.

The important thing was he realized, as all patients must realize, that while I can make people look better, given their age or physical circumstance, their destiny is in their own hands, not mine. I have no idea whether that fellow ever did go out into the meet market, or whether he stayed home and watched television, but whatever he did, thanks to facial cosmetic surgery, he looked a little better doing it.

So now that I've introduced myself and told you a bit about my profession, let's talk about you, the potential patient.

The Facial Assessment

THE FIRST ORDER OF BUSINESS, once I've established that a patient is a good candidate for facial cosmetic surgery, is to find out what the chief complaint is. We get to this easily enough: I simply say, "What's bothering you?" The answer is not always so straightforward. A patient might tell me that she doesn't like the bump on the end of her nose, but her idea of where the end of her nose is could be different from mine. I'll make the patient point with a finger directly at the area of concern, and sometimes, it's a surprise to me.

One reason I can be surprised is that, naturally, I take a more objective view of a patient's face than the patient is able to. It's not as simple as "A nose is a nose is a nose" (with apologies to Gertrude Stein).

Balance and Proportion

In a facial assessment, I start by looking for balance, or lack of balance, as the case may be. To do this, I mentally draw lines that would divide the face roughly into three parts: the top third extends from your forehead hairline to the middle of your eyebrows; the middle third is from your eyebrows to the base of your nose; and the bottom third is from the base of your nose to the lower edge of the chin. If the three parts are essentially equal in height, you've got a nicely proportioned face, no matter what your individual features might look like to you.

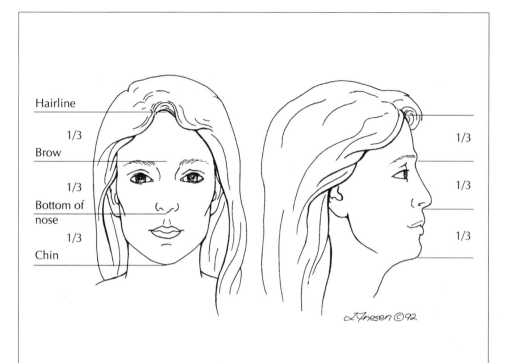

When assessing a face, I divide it into three parts. In an ideally proportioned face, these parts will be essentially equal in height.

But let's just say that the bottom third of your face is noticeably shorter than the top two-thirds. Perhaps you have a slightly receding chin. While all you can see is the bump on your nose, I can see that once I've reduced the overall size of your nose, perhaps as a result of minimizing the bump, I'll have to add a small chin augmentation, a "chin implant" as it is called, in order to balance the effect.

Or my assessment of your chief concern might have less to do with overall balance than with a slight deviation that you haven't been able to properly identify. To continue with the example of the bump on your nose, it could be that the natural aging process or upper-teeth dental surgery has caused the nose to drop its tip a bit, and as a result, a bump on the dorsum (the central ridge of the nose), has begun to appear. The solution might have more to do with tilting the tip up than smoothing out a bump. I have a three-way mirror in my office, and I have my patient to stand in front of it so we can consider balance and profile, letting his or her face illustrate our discussion.

The Possibilities

The thing to remember as you learn more about the facial assessment, and about some of the corrective procedures outlined in this book, is that the art of facial cosmetic surgery is essentially the art of disguise. It's not so much that I can actually "change" your face, but that I can minimize the problems of aging, disfiguration and balance, so that the overall effect is more pleasing. And I can only change what you give me to work with, which is *your own face*. I've had patients come in and give me the photograph of a model from a magazine, demanding a

Patients are often surprised to discover that the root of their concern lies in a simple lack of balance. Note the small chin and the shortened bottom third on the left and the shortened upper third on the right.

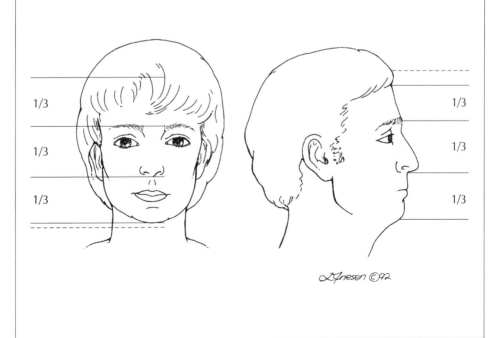

1/3		1/3
1/3		1/3
1/3		1/3

similar nose to hers, or his, and it can't be done, unless they've got that kind of nose to start with.

A good example of the kind of disguise I'm talking about, or visual illusion, is when a patient with deep acne scarring comes to me. First I do a facial assessment under direct, fluorescent lighting, to see exactly where the light catches the edges of the scars to cast shadows. My surgical approach will be to minimize those areas by planing them down, or using other methods, so that light playing on the face is reflected more evenly and the skin appears to be smoother. If it is warranted and the patient agrees, I might take the imaginative step of recommending eyelid surgery and/or a brow-lift, so that when the patient is fully healed, the troublesome skin seems less evident and the expressive eyes are suddenly more noticeable.

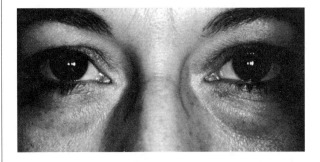

If a patient has loose skin and fatty deposits around her eyes, they will be more obvious when she leans forward and looks up.

Once we've agreed on the area of chief concern, be it a bump on the nose or something else, then I'll start to educate the patient with regard to the balance we seek. I point out the options, and the routes we might take. For example, if I notice, during assessment of the nose, that the patient has a deep line between the eyebrows at the top of the nose due to frowning, I might suggest a collagen injection to smooth it out. Or if I see that the patient's main problem is that natural aging has caused the forehead to drop, I can suggest we lift it — partly because it will enhance the nose job, and partly because, as I have said, I strive for balance in a face as much as possible. As a patient, however, you should know that you don't have to follow all of your surgeon's suggestions. There is always the option of doing nothing at all.

Sometimes the options I suggest are dictated by the patient's age and heredity. For example, I have a couple of simple techniques to test for loose skin that has lost its elasticity around the eyes. These techniques tell me if surgery will make a difference to the patient's appearance. First I'll ask the patient to tilt her head forward, so that she is looking up into a mirror. Loose skin and fatty deposits under the eyes become immediately more apparent this way, and I'll pull gently on the skin with a tiny pair of forceps or my fingers to illustrate exactly what I am talking about. With the patient's head upright, I'll take the same forceps and pull on the skin above the eyes to check again for looseness. Usually, the excessive skin or "draping" of upper lids is due to age but sometimes heredity is the cause and it can appear in a patient's twenties.

This kind of facial assessment also allows me to take special note of the way a patient reacts to my use of the forceps. Most are a little jumpy at first, naturally, but if a nervous reaction persists, I have cause for concern. One of the elements of facial cosmetic surgery that sets it apart from other types of surgery is that it is elective, meaning the patient has voluntarily sought it out. This should mean that there is less apprehension and reluctance on the part of the patient.

It is important that facial cosmetic surgery patients are comfortable with touching, because many of the procedures are performed

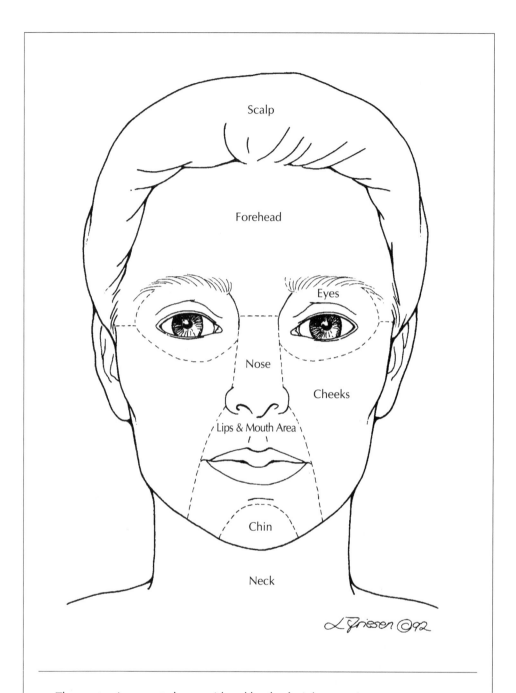

Scalp

Forehead

Eyes

Nose

Cheeks

Lips & Mouth Area

Chin

Neck

The anatomic areas to be considered by the facial cosmetic surgeon are divided into the eight regional aesthetic units.

under a local anesthetic and with intravenous sedation. I can't have someone flinching on the operating table just because I'm working close to the eye or have moved in close to the face. And, during some procedures, I rely on what the touch of my fingers tells me; often I am operating underneath the skin, so that I have to feel for results rather than look for them. This would be the case, for example, with a liposuction of the neck. Finally, a patient must be comfortable with touching for the follow-up procedures. Sometimes I have to remove stitches. Often I'll palpate the area I've worked on — touch it and move it around gently with my fingers — to check the healing process. If you're squeamish about having your face touched, you are not a good candidate for this kind of surgery.

Another consideration during an assessment is the age of a patient, which can influence both the procedures and the results of surgery. I might be looking for slack skin that needs reduction in an older patient, but with regard to rhinoplasty (surgery for the nose) and otoplasty (surgery for flyaway ears), youth is an important consideration. Otoplasty can be done any time after a child reaches four years of age, but there are other factors to take into account. For one, I have to use a general anesthetic on young patients; they can't be expected to lie quietly on an operating table. For another, the follow-up procedure with otoplasty requires that the patient wear a light, around-the-ear hairband for about two weeks after surgery, and some young children are not able to do this.

As for young people and rhinoplasty, my first concern is whether or not the patient has stopped growing. Some kids stop as young as fourteen, others don't stop until they're sixteen or even older. If I operate on a youngster who hasn't stopped growing, the growth centers of the nose might be damaged, or affected, and the nose will continue to grow, but in an odd way. For the ten-year-old whose nose has been bashed in a school-yard fight, I can do a preliminary operation to keep the bones and cartilage as straight as possible for pre-pubertal growth spurt. Then we wait until the child stops growing before doing the final cosmetic work.

After we've agreed on the work to be done during the facial assessment, I try to illustrate exactly how I will do it. I start by introducing patients to the eight "regional aesthetic units" of the face — all anatomic areas that must be considered separately by the cosmetic surgeon: scalp, forehead, eyes, cheeks, nose, lips and mouth area, chin, and neck. I have a number of illustrative aids, such as before-and-after photographs, medical texts with detailed drawings, some slides of previous patients, and even pen and paper. I've prepared sheets of paper with the outline of a face on it so that I can make notes about the assessment for future reference. As I mentioned before, I can "see" three-dimensionally, so I make use of a miniature plaster face with a cutaway section to show a patient what will happen under the skin during an operation. (I was once challenged by an artist to produce a Plasticine facial sculpture, and sure enough, I found it easy to do, but the ability to sketch a face on paper is beyond me. I can't draw worth a bean.)

Part of the reason I go to such lengths to illustrate the process is to instill confidence in my patient. A patient offering up his face must know that he can trust his surgeon to stay with him, even if complications arise. And they do. The law of averages dictates that if I do one hundred rhinoplasties, a certain percentage of them will give me trouble. This is what I meant by making sure that you get along well with your surgeon. If, despite all the planning, an unforeseen problem comes up — the cartilage in your nose twists due to the return of its intrinsic "spring" (this might happen if the nose was damaged in an accident) or if there is persistent post operative swelling due to delayed healing — your surgeon must be there for you. The rule of thumb here is, don't be afraid of a doctor who tells you about all the things that might go wrong, because they just might.

You should come out of a facial assessment session with a pretty good idea of the price you'll have to pay for your surgery, and money isn't the only currency. In the appendix at the back of this book you'll find some guidelines as to what you might spend on various procedures, but there are some other considerations. Pain, for example. With modern anesthetics, there is no cause for pain during any procedure, outside of a pinprick sensation during the "freezing" or numbing injections, but there can be uncomfortable periods during healing. The good news is that you'll rarely need anything more powerful than Tylenol 3 to deal with it, and that some patients experience no pain but only pressure or tightness during healing.

Generally speaking, even the most extensive facial plastic surgery — for example a rhinoplasty — allows you to be socially active in about two weeks. There will be some colorful bruising and swelling in the meantime, but after two weeks, often with no makeup, you should be able to go to a party and no one will know you've had your nose done, unless you tell them. Some operations do require follow-up procedures like wearing headbands or chin slings for a while, which I'll elaborate on in the relevant chapters.

The thing to remember is that the true healing process, below the skin, takes much longer than two weeks. In the case of a rhinoplasty, it takes about a year. You and your doctor need to arrange a schedule of follow-up appointments over this longer period of time to make sure everything is healing the way it should.

A thorough facial assessment, then, is an essential first step toward facial cosmetic surgery. It should lay to rest any myths or misconceptions you might harbor about what can or must be done. You should walk out of an assessment fully confident that you know exactly what is going to be done, why and how it is to be done, how much it will cost, when it will be done, and over what period of time it will heal. You'll probably also have found out some fascinating new things about yourself, just by the way you interact with your surgeon and the way you respond to his probing and assessment of that most personal calling card — your face.

And now, let's talk about skin.

Aging Skin

AGING OF THE SKIN, which we'll deal with in this chapter, is a constantly changing process that is controlled by both intrinsic and extrinsic factors. In an article I wrote for *The Canadian Journal of Diagnosis*, with Dr. Eric Gage, we put the three main skin problems caused by aging — hollowing, sagging and wrinkling — into perspective, and I'll share some of the less-technical information with you here.

Factors That Age the Skin

The effects of aging are less apparent in people with relatively dark, thick, oily skin — characteristics that are often determined by heredity and race. It is interesting that the blond cheerleader who was admired so much in high school for her flawless skin probably will age at a much faster rate than her olive-skinned, dark-haired classmate who was barely noticed. Of course, a patient's general health and nutritional habits, as well as smoking and exposure to the sun, affect the aging process. So do sudden physical changes: for example, people who lose a lot of weight in a short time often appear to be much older.

Though everyone ages at an individual rate, you'll notice some plateaus when aging is gradual, and periods when the aging process

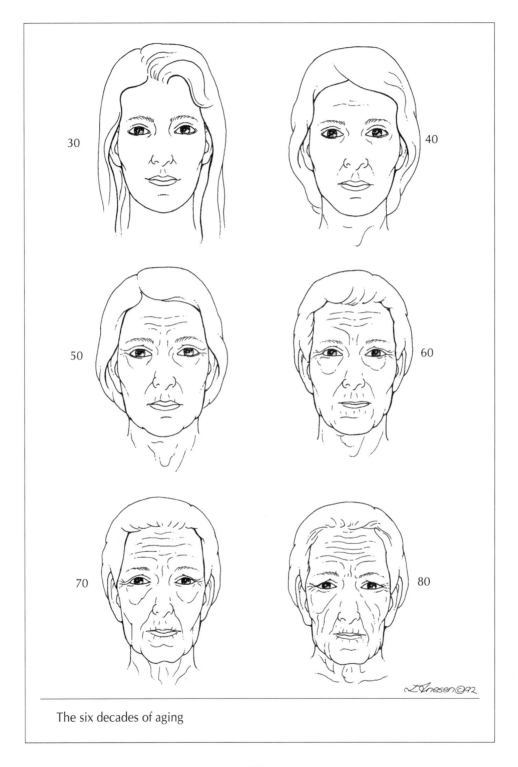

The six decades of aging

is accelerated. At twenty-five, you'll notice the beginning of lip-cheek grooves that, by about thirty, will reach the corners of your mouth. At forty, you'll start to gain a few lines on the forehead and under the eyes. At fifty, a few more lines will form in these same areas. Between fifty and sixty, there is an accelerated period of aging when all of the lines become more evident, and some sagging starts. Then there is a reprieve from sixty to seventy when you coast along without much change. Between seventy-five and eighty, the process accelerates rapidly, and this is when you literally appear to "shrivel" with age.

Extrinsic factors such as wind or the sun's ultraviolet rays accelerate aging in exposed skin. Usually, it is facial skin that is most damaged: skiers, golfers and farmers often suffer premature aging of the face. Smoking accelerates aging by affecting the supply of oxygen to the blood. (Some heavy smokers in their early thirties complain about vertical wrinkles in their upper lip, but there is no proven connection to the constant pursing of lips around a cigarette.)

How Skin Ages

It helps to know a bit about how skin is constructed to understand how it ages. When I work with skin on the operating table, it reminds me of handling pie pastry, because of its texture and the way you have to lift and maneuvre it. But my metaphor wouldn't produce a particularly good pie because skin is astoundingly tough. People think of skin as a thin, delicate sheath, but that is true of only a few places, like the upper and lower eyelids. Also, skin is slightly stretchable in some other places, like the cheeks and jowls. Young interns are always surprised at how vigorously we are able to work underneath the skin during a liposuction without fear of tearing.

Skin is composed of a fine upper layer called the epidermis, and a thicker layer underneath called the dermis. (On top of the epidermis is a layer of dead cells called the stratum corneum, or keratin.) The thickness of the dermis varies with each individual, and also varies according to its location on the body. For example, eyelid dermis is much thinner than dermis elsewhere. The dermis, together with a subcutaneous layer of tissue below, houses essential features like

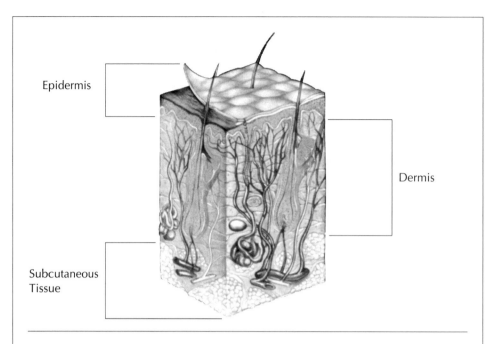

Epidermis

Dermis

Subcutaneous
Tissue

Anatomy of skin

sebaceous tissue, including glands that secrete oil for lubricating hair and skin, hair follicles, sweat glands, fatty tissue and proteins like elastin and collagen. Collagen gives strength to the skin.

Skin, combined with its subcutaneous layer, is the protective slip between our internal organs... and the big, wide world. Fred Allen, the American editor and historian, once said about skin, the body's largest and often least-appreciated organ: "To a newspaperman, a human being is an item with the skin wrapped around it." He wasn't far wrong.

When young, the skin is smooth, moist-looking and shiny, with a kind of brilliant sheen. The "glow," or sheen, is due to another kind of protein which is smooth and regular, called keratin, atop the epidermis. As it ages, this layer of keratin becomes irregular, and, depending on the factors such as heredity and exposure to sun that I've outlined above, the skin will appear dry, less shiny and even scaly.

The aging process also thins the dermis layer of skin more than the epidermis, beginning at about age thirty-five in women and age forty-five in men. (The thinner the skin, the earlier it wrinkles, which is why wrinkling often begins with the eyelids.) Postmenopausally in women, and at about age fifty-five in men, the sebaceous, oil-producing glands in the dermis and subcutaneous layers begin to atrophy, or waste away. And finally, the dermis begins to lose structural support as proteins like collagen and elastin begin to change form and atrophy.

Hollowing

Of the three main problems associated with aging of the skin, hollowing is the most easily explainable. It is a phenomenon associated with the late aging process and is a direct result of the wasting away or atrophy of fat under the bottom layer of skin, the subcutaneous tissue. When it happens in the areas of cheek or temple, or both, it creates a skeletal, sunken appearance.

Hollowing results when the fat in the subcutaneous tissue of the skin in the mid-face region wastes away during the aging process.

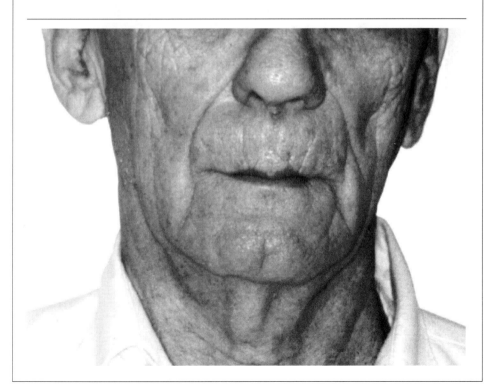

Mid-cheek hollowing, just below the cheekbone, is usually associated with elderly people in their seventies and beyond, or with people who have very high cheekbones. Mid-cheek hollowing can also occur in people who naturally have very little fat in their cheeks. The problem shows up when they are in their forties and fifties. The cheek fat, or buccal fat as it is known, shrinks — giving the face a gaunt, haggard look. Some patients who suffer from this are perpetually sad looking. But hollowing can be easily corrected in the mid-cheek area with a silicone implant — a procedure known as submalar augmentation. The implants come in various shapes and sizes to create the best possible effect for the patient. Unlike the material used in silicone breast implants, this silicone is solid.

Hollowing can also become apparent in people who suffer a grave illness. I once had a patient who was dying of ovarian cancer. To keep her spirits up over what turned out to be the last year of her life, she wanted to look in the mirror and see a healthy-looking face. In this case, I simply injected her at intervals with massive doses of collagen.

Another kind of hollowing can occur as a result of shrinkage around the "alveolar process" — the bony ridge containing the sockets of the teeth. Bony atrophy is often a result of having teeth capped or removing the upper four front teeth, and it can cause the nasal tip to droop. When the bone begins to waste away, the orbicularis oris muscle, the round muscle that encircles the lips, will shorten. In this area of the face, the skin is attached directly to the muscle, and so the shortening causes vertical lines around the lips, a bit like a collapsed accordian.

Sagging

The second main problem people have when they age is that their skin "sags." Sagging in the lower face produces a jowly effect. Not only does the skin stretch, but the subcutaneous fat falls, producing jowls and giving the lower face a square appearance. There are several reasons for this, the first and most obvious being gravity. Skin is an envelope that stretches with time and gravity. However, the contents of this envelope shrink due to fat atrophy and the absorption of bone, so the skin sags. The effect of gravity can be most evident in the brow area. Ordinarily, the eyebrows should lie atop the bony orbit surrounding the eyes — call it the escarpment of the forehead. With age, the forehead might sag so that the brows drop below the escarpment.

Sagging in the lower half of the face becomes noticeable gradually as people age through their late forties. This has less to do with gravity than it does with the SMAS fascia. SMAS is an acronym for the Superficial Musculo-Aponeurotic System; fascia is an anatomical expression for a sheath of connective tissue that binds or supports internal organs (in a sense, skin is also a fascia). In the face, the SMAS fascia is a delicate kind of sinew that lies beneath the deepest layer of skin. It separates the skin from the underlying glands and

The SMAS fascia is a sheath of connective tissue that lies under the deepest layer of skin; as it ages, the fascia loses its elasticity.

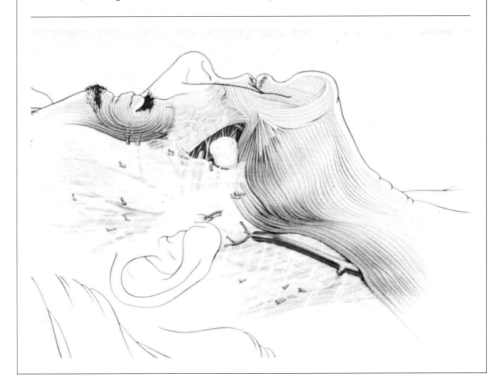

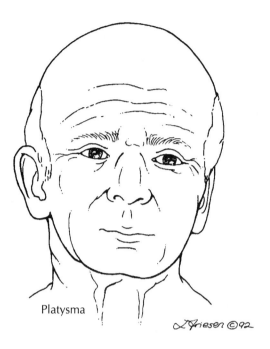

Platysma

As we age, the platysma muscle also sags forward, creating two cords in the front of the neck.

the muscles that produce facial expressions. To get a mental picture of the SMAS fascia, think about an embryonic sac, or membrane. As it ages, the SMAS fascia loses its elasticity, just the way the elastic waistline in your favorite old pair of pants begins to give way.

When the SMAS fascia begins to sag with age, the sagging can cause several noticeable changes in the face. People with an already-deep crease in the lip-cheek groove might find it is made more pronounced by a fleshy fold of skin that results in what we call the "hill and valley" phenomenon — where the valley is the groove and the hill is the lateral cheek mound. Or a person might begin to develop jowls, which are essentially fat-filled pockets of skin that hang below the normal jawline. Sometimes jowls are made more noticeable when a person is overweight, but often even a perfectly natural amount of fat will hang simply because the SMAS fascia and skin have lost their elasticity. When someone is overweight, the extra fat combined with a loose SMAS fascia can create both a jowly look and a double chin.

The neck can also be affected by the SMAS fascia because it is directly connected, or structurally continuous, with the platysma. The platysma is a broad, thin muscle on either side of the neck that extends from the top part of each shoulder all the way up over either side of the jawbone. (Try stretching your neck, then grimacing with your jaw clenched and the lower teeth showing, and you'll see the outline of the platysma.) This is the muscle that causes wrinkling in the neck — the horizontal lines are caused by the folding of the skin due to the pull of gravity and the platysma muscle. The front edge of the muscle causes cording in the front of the neck and the wrinkles occur perpendicularly to the direction of muscle pull.

When facial cosmetic surgeons first began to perfect the art of the face-lift, it was common to simply pull back the skin without addressing underlying problems like the sagging SMAS fascia. As a result, the operation often didn't last more than a couple of years. Today, depending on when a patient has a face-lift, it is possible to get satisfactory results for a much longer period of time because we can do a double-layer face-lift operation that deals separately with both the SMAS fascia and the skin.

Wrinkling

I have a certain fondness for wrinkling as the third most common skin problem associated with aging. This is partly because a patient's wrinkles tell me something of their personality, and partly because there are several, imaginative solutions available with which to deal with wrinkles.

As mentioned above, the degree of wrinkling varies with a patient's heredity and race. I see many more fair-skinned patients for wrinkling than I do black, Oriental or olive-skinned Caucasian patients. The thicker and oilier the skin, the less likely it is to wrinkle. And, as noted, thin skin wrinkles faster than thick skin. That said, there are certain personality traits that also affect wrinkling.

In simple terms, the wrinkle pattern that appears in the upper half of the face is caused by squinters, frowners and eyebrow lifters. These are the only three movements that the forehead can produce. Any of these habitual facial expressions can begin as early as age six in some people, so you can imagine how entrenched some wrinkle patterns become.

Squinters end up with "crow's feet," wrinkles resembling the shape and texture of bird's feet, around the outer corners of the eye. Sometimes, people squint due to long-term, uncorrected problems with eyesight, and I've also seen crow's feet on scholars who are compulsive readers. Chronic frowners, on the other hand, develop glabellar frown lines, named for the glabella, or flat area of bone between the eyebrows. These are small, often deep, vertical lines between the eyes. But the most common upper facial expression is eyebrow lifting, which causes horizontal wrinkling of the forehead.

The wrinkle pattern in our upper faces is caused by the only three movements the forehead can make: squinting, frowning, and eyebrow lifting.

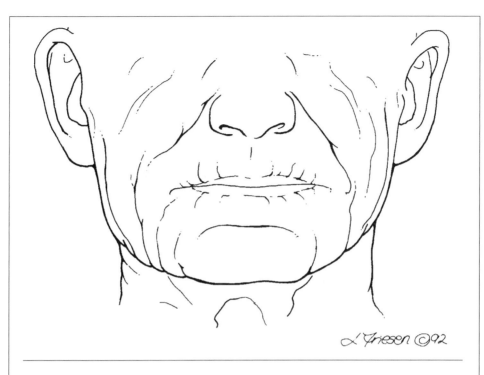

In the lower half of the face, wrinkles are concentrated around the lip area; in the lip-cheek grooves, and spread into the cheek/jowl area.

In a study I completed in 1988 with Dr. Haitham Masri, we found that statistics indicate that forty-eight percent of people are predominantly eyebrow raisers, while thirty-five percent are chronic frowners. Of course, no one uses a single type of facial expressive movement, so there are blends of wrinkle patterns.

In the lower half of the face, wrinkling generally appears in two distinct areas. We've discussed before the vertical wrinkles that can appear around the mouth. This wrinkling is usually caused by bony atrophy, or hollowing.

The second area is in the lip-cheek groove, one of the boundaries that separates the eight "regional aesthetic units" of the face. (See Chapter One: The Facial Assessment.) The lip-cheek groove, which starts out as a shallow line at the juncture of the two units, deepens with age and becomes particularly pronounced in thin-skinned people during their thirties and forties.

Surface Skin Techniques

Vitamin A Acid Cream

There has been a major breakthrough within the past five years with the age-diminishing Vitamin A Acid Cream, sold by prescription under a variety of brand names. Dermatologists began to use the cream to stabilize or stop the worst of the eruption of skin traumatized by acne, and in the treatment of precancerous lesions. They noticed that patients who used the cream for a lengthy period of time, up to a year or longer, actually managed to retard and reverse some of the natural process of aging.

Applied nightly, Vitamin A Acid Cream thins the dead cell layer of skin, which gives the skin a moisturized appearance. It's relatively inexpensive and not very glamorous yet, but there is no doubt that it is remarkably effective for some people. Most of the commercial anti-aging creams on the market today do little more than cause temporary swelling of the superficial dead cell layer, which visually smooths out wrinkles for a time. But Vitamin A Acid Cream gradually changes the cellular maturation of the epidermal layer of skin, giving the skin a more youthful appearance. Over a long period of time, months or years, it is reputed to lay down extra collagen within the dermis.

Before you charge into the local drugstore to demand a tube, you must get a prescription and be warned that a dangerous side effect of Vitamin A Acid Cream is that it could make your skin hypersensitive to the sun and ultraviolet radiation. Sunbathing, or even accidentally remaining in the sun for extensive periods of time while picnicking or watching a baseball game, might result in a severe skin reaction. Users have to make a decision between getting a tan, or using the cream. During the summer months, a broad spectrum sunscreen with an SPF (sun protection factor) greater than 15 must be worn at all times. I wouldn't recommend that you start a regimen with Vitamin A Acid Cream without first checking with your doctor.

I have a large number of patients on Vitamin A Acid Cream, and it is useful to know that about one-third of them love it and use it every day, one-third think it's a waste of time, and one-third have a neutral opinion about it. The difference among them might be explained by the fact that a patient has got to be obsessive about applying it diligently every single night before bed. Chances are, if a patient doesn't already have the habit of using a night cream, the results from Vitamin A Acid Cream will be less than satisfactory.

A new type of cream made from "fruit acids" is now available and has fewer side effects than Vitamin A Acid Cream. The active ingredient is glycolic acid in an eight to ten percent concentration. This cream works on the superficial dead cell layer of skin and the epidermis, smoothing the skin's surface. Coupled with light, superficial and refreshing peels made of a higher concentration of glycolic acid, this cream can reduce the effects of wrinkling and aging.

Nonsurgical Face-lifts

Another age-diminishing, or so-called age-diminishing, item on the market these days is the "nonsurgical" face-lift. Often you'll see it advertised at spas or upscale beauty salons. A nonsurgical face-lift, administered by aestheticians, is essentially a procedure whereby electrical currents are applied to the muscles of the face. It seems to me to be an adaptation of the popular muscle stimulators that athletes use for muscle toning, which spas have applied to the thighs and rumps of people who can't be bothered exercising.

I investigated the procedure several years ago with a control group of patients, but I didn't see any discernible difference in their before-and-after pictures, even after six months of treatment. There are solid, physiological reasons why simply toning the muscles of the face won't alter anything — the sag of the SMAS fascia for example — but still, nonsurgical face-lifts are gaining in popularity. To my mind, perhaps nonsurgical face-lifts, as well as commercial anti-aging creams, might provide temporary results of a minor nature.

Injection Treatments

Depending on how deep the wrinkling is, and whether or not the patient has the desire to correct other signs of aging, I can apply a couple of solutions to the problem. If the wrinkling is deep, the patient will often have other noticeable aging details, like cording in the neck. In this case, we would consider a general face-lift, a subject I deal with in a later chapter on face-lifts (Chapter Six). A face-lift can reduce even the deepest groove by about fifty percent. If the groove is reasonably shallow, I can inject collagen. (The same thing I might do with the small vertical lines that frowners get between their eyes, or with small lines around the eyes or mouth.)

If the groove is deeper, I'd be inclined to insert Gore-Tex (expanded polytetrafluoroethylene). Cosmetic surgeons now use it instead of an injectable filler. For lip-cheek grooves, it is surgically implanted while the patient is under a local anaesthetic. Gore-Tex creates a good foundation, making the grooves more shallow. Further correction of the problem is then made with collagen injections if necessary.

Silicone was an early and popular injectable filler. It is a manufactured polymer containing silicon and oxygen atoms; it is used as an adhesive, a lubricant, as a hydraulic oil and in electrical insulation, as well as in cosmetics and cosmetic surgery. It can take several forms — fluid, resinous, rubbery or firm — depending on various factors like the arrangement of the silicon atoms and temperature. The silicone I have used, for example, has a viscosity of 1,000 centistrokes. When you push it through a needle, it is clear, with the consistency of liquid honey, or maple syrup.

When silicone was first introduced about fifteen years ago, the problem was that cosmetic surgeons were just learning to use it. Some injected far too much of it, and patients ended up with hard, permanent ridges under their skin. Other surgeons injected it in a helter-skelter fashion, without realizing the consequences, and patients ended up with ridges or scalloped areas of the face; it felt like subcutaneous corduroy to the touch. During my internship, I saw an instance where a patient had had an injection of exceptionally thin, watery silicone (say, twenty-eight centistrokes), and it all ran down to the end of her nose and formed a ball.

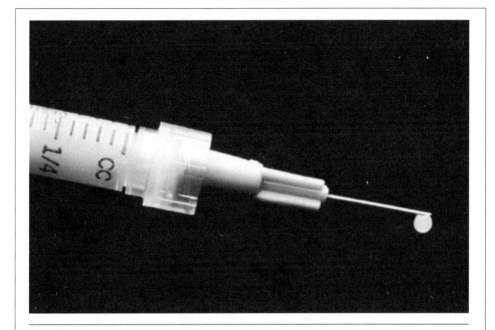

Collagen is a biological product that makes an ideal three-dimensional injectable filler for treating human skin.

Today, although we know much more about the handling of silicone, there is still some danger from injecting too much. For this reason, I generally favor the injection of manufactured collagen. As I mentioned before, collagen is present naturally in the dermis layer of skin, but the material we inject is "manufactured" from the skin, or hide, of cows.

Under a microscope, human collagen looks like cotton wool with fibres in alpha-helical folds — a biological structuring that resembles the coils of a Slinky toy. Collagen gives the skin strength and bulk. To manufacture collagen, The Collagen Corporation of California purified the biological composition of cowhide so that it resembled human collagen, then mixed it with a local anesthetic fluid. (Koken, a Japanese company, has a similar product.) Collagen looks and feels a bit like tapioca or toothpaste, and if you rub it between your fingers, it will form into tiny, sticky balls. When it is injected, the combination of elements at room temperature solidifies into a filler — what we call a "three-dimensional volume implant" — ideal for the treatment of human skin.

I like collagen because it allows the use of much finer needles. Injections with finer needles are much less painful. I can use a number 30 needle with collagen — a needle almost as fine as a hair — but I have to use at least a number 26 with silicone. (For comparative purposes, the finest needle is number 30, the thickest is number 16. Laid side by the side, the number 16 almost looks like a gardening implement; medical labs use a number 22 to draw blood samples.) Naturally, there are some drawbacks with either product: collagen disperses in the body as a biological product, which makes it safer than silicone, but this requires return visits for continuing injections every three to six months.

Peels

There is another kind of wrinkling that has little to do with personality, or even heredity, unless you apply those factors to the case of the blond, fine-skinned patient who stubbornly insists on spending a great deal of time in the sun without sunscreen protection. By the time this patient reaches the late-forties, serious sun damage will begin to show in the form of a kind of "spiderweb," or fine etching, often on the eyelids and cheeks. Happily, we are able to treat this patient with a chemical peel that, in many cases, can remove up to ninety percent of the wrinkling. It is important to remember that a chemical peel is best for wrinkles that affect the texture of the skin, not wrinkles caused by habitual facial expression.

According to a medical text on the subject, published as a guide for facial plastic surgeons by the American Academy of Facial Plastic and Reconstructive Surgery, the chemical peel, or "chemexfoliation" as it is technically known, was invented by an otolaryngologist named Sir Harold Gillies. He used carbolic acid, known as phenol, as an agent to decrease the elasticity of aged eyelid skin. Since then, various other acids, such as trichloroacetic and glycolic acid, have been used in efforts to improve the texture of skin, but phenol has come through as the most effective agent for deeper skin problems.

Chemical peel solution can be divided into three types, depending on the depth to which the peel penetrates. Phenol, the deepest of peels, removes all the epidermis and part of the top of the dermis, working to smooth the skin within the dermis layer. Phenol is good for the treatment of eyelid wrinkling and skin tightening, and it works well on problems associated with over-exposure to the sun.

For epidermal problems such as freckles, liver spots, melasma — dark skin spots that appear during pregnancy — age spots, and post-inflammatory hyperpigmentation, a trichloroacetic acid peel (TCA peel, for short) works best. TCA peels come in various concentrations, but thirty-five percent strength solution will solve most of the problems I've mentioned. A deeper TCA peel can be used to treat fine wrinkling.

A fifty percent glycolic acid peel, is the most superficial peel. It generally is used for exfoliation that renews the keratin layer of skin, giving the face a refreshed look. This sort of treatment can be applied regularly, along with glycolic acid cream applied twice daily. Frequent glycolic acid peels fade age spots and improve areas of wrinkling. (With this peel, you can go to a party the same day of the peel — the face has only a hint of pink.)

The deep chemical peel formula, which is applied with a cotton-tip swab, is composed of eighty-eight percent phenol, croton oil, antiseptic soap and distilled water. I've given the recipe only to illustrate the delicacy of the technique: essentially, a chemical peel is a controlled acid burn. Croton oil, from the seed of *Croton tiglium*, is composed of glycerides of several acids, and it is a very toxic material. Croton oil combined with phenol effectively dissolves the epidermis. The liquid soap, such as Septisol, has several functions, like increasing the penetration of the phenol and croton oil into the deeper layers of the skin. It also makes the phenol and water mix with one another. The distilled water produces the correct chemical concentration of the mixture so that penetration can be controlled.

With a full-face chemical peel, the formula is applied more or less the way you'd apply a facial or mud mask. From time to time, I perform full-face peels in the Toronto area where I practice, but doctors who practice in the Sun Belt latitudes of the U.S. would be more likely to do them regularly because of the number of patients who've spent a lifetime in the sun. In Southern Ontario, most people are wise enough to use sunscreens; even farmers work in air-conditioned tractors these days. Most often, I do regional peels, so-called for the eight aesthetic units of the face. For example, I can use a regional chemical peel on the crow's feet at the corner of a patient's eye. A peel also works well on the etched wrinkles that sometimes appear on the lower eyelid or on the so-called "lipstick" wrinkles — the wrinkles where lipstick settles into embarrassing vertical lines — of the upper lip.

As effective as it is, there are drawbacks to the phenol chemical peel. For one, it actually lightens the color of the skin. This means it has to be applied with a feathering motion around the edges — for example, at the hairline, around the ears and slightly into the vermilion of the lips — or the patient may end up with an obvious line of demarcation where the paler skin meets the darker. This lightening effect makes it a difficult technique to use with black or olive-skinned people. For a period of time following the peel, patients have a pinkness added to their skin color though the contrast does, eventually, fade. The new skin is smoother with slightly less pigmentation than before. Rock star Michael Jackson is reputed to have had a series of full-face chemical peels to permanently lighten the color of his skin, which, in my opinion, is a questionable use of the phenol chemical-peel technique.

During application of a chemical-peel solution, it's important that a patient's tears do not touch the solution. Tears might be caused by the temporary stinging or burning sensation that follows contact with the skin. If the solution tracks into the eye, it will cause severe burns to the eyeball. As the solution acts on the skin, a kind of white frost develops as the chemicals begin to burn. About ten minutes after application, the burning sensation stops and then may return within the next six or seven hours, when some sort of pain-killing medication might be required. Eight hours after application, most of the pain will disappear, though there is a lingering discomfort for some days due to the swelling of the skin in the area peeled.

The day after the operation, the skin becomes gray in color and "edematous," or pooled with liquid, just like a burn. It will show the first signs of peeling. On the second day, the skin looks even worse, more liquidy and more swollen. If it has been a regional peel in the area of the eyes, or the lips, it is likely that the eyes might swell nearly shut, or the lips will puff up like a boxer's. For the next two weeks, a patient may shower daily and then cover the peeled areas with Polysporin ointment.

Somewhere between the seventh and tenth day after application, the crusting and peeling skin is completely shed. This is the stage when the patient must expect to wear a bright red face, or bright red patches if I've done regional peels. The new healing skin is very delicate, and the temptation to pick away final little bits of crust must be avoided: essentially, the patient has experienced a second-degree burn, and picking will cause infection that might result in scarring. The showering and lubricating allows the crust to be shed naturally without a great amount of itching or discomfort.

A phenol chemical peel is an effective treatment of the severe spiderweb wrinkles caused by sun damage.

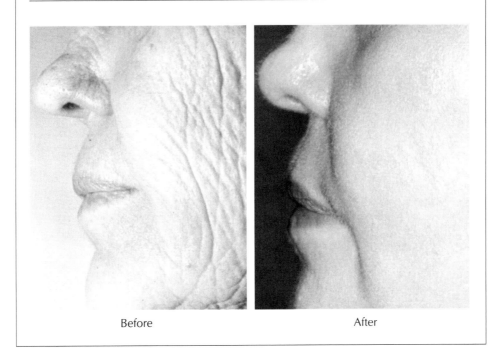

Before   After

Within the next month, the bright red skin will fade to an intense pink and then lesser shades of pink as the healing process continues. At no time, for six months following the operation, should the skin be exposed to direct sunlight. Even if you plan to travel in a car on a sunny day, your new skin must be covered with a broad spectrum sunscreen that has an SPF of at least 15. The chemical peel is used to correct damage done by overexposure to the sun. Perhaps it is a kind of cruel retribution for past excesses that if a patient exposes the new skin to the sun, it may result in hyperpigmentation — blotchy, brown spots that might require a lighter re-peel.

I have not spared anything in this description of the process and postoperative effects of the chemical peel because it is a gruesome sort of ordeal, and no matter how much I try to prepare patients for it, the sight in the mirror is always a shock to them. It's important for them to know the steps that must be gone through in order to get a good effect.

It might be some comfort to know that at the end of two weeks, some patients are healed sufficiently to actually apply water-based makeup. This gives women a slight advantage over men in that they can "go public" a little faster. With the less penetrating TCA peels, patients have fewer reactions and are "socially acceptable" in seven days. As noted earlier, with the glycolic acid peels, patients can go out the same day; their faces have an acceptable glow. These days more patients choose the lighter peels for a more youthful appearance without going through the deeper phenol peels.

Despite the ordeal, chemical peel is a dramatically effective technique for dealing with some of the consequences of aging skin. I sometimes think of it as lifting the mask of age to reveal a patient's more youthful face.

It is a fortunate era for facial cosmetic surgeons like myself to have such nearly magical tools at our fingertips: our patients need look only as old as they want to.

CHAPTER THREE

The Eye Region

FOR SOME REASON, people often come looking for a blepharoplasty, or plastic surgery of the eye, when they are having romantic troubles. As I explained in the chapter on facial assessment (Chapter One), I have to proceed carefully in these cases because patients are setting themselves up for disappointment if they think removing the bags under their eyes will win back a lost love. Knowing this doesn't shield me from their tears, however, and I am truly saddened by some of the stories I hear. The advice I give to the man or woman whose spouse has just run off is go home, dry their tears and come to see me again in six months, when they are more emotionally stable.

Recently, I thought I had properly screened a patient, and we went ahead with both a face-lift and a blepharoplasty. She had casually mentioned that her husband was away for three weeks and that a girlfriend would be coming to take her home after the operation. Over the course of several, subsequent postoperative visits, I finally found out that her husband had, indeed, left her. If I'd known, I very likely wouldn't have taken her on, but she proved the exception to the rule and handled the breakup well. I was less gullible with a fellow who came in and said, "Do my eyes, Doc. My wife and I have split up." We waited for a while on that one.

Simply put, blepharoplasty is an operation that removes the excess skin and fat of the upper and/or lower eyelids. The excess skin comes about because, with age, the thin skin of the eyelids loses its elasticity and begins to sag. A blepharoplasty makes the eyes look larger and even gives them more sparkle — quite literally, I think, because the surface area of the cornea, the "window" of the eye, catches more light.

Upper and Lower Lid Surgery

The blepharoplasty procedure is generally referred to as upper or lower blepharoplasty, relating to the upper or lower eyelids. Quite often, a patient will assume the need for an upper blepharoplasty when, in fact, the excessive skin of the upper eyelids can be corrected with a forehead-lift, which I describe later in this chapter. There

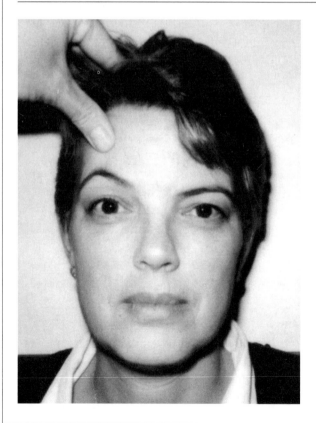

Both an upper blepharopasty and a forehead lift will create a more wide-eyed look. As shown here, a forehead lift achieves this by simply raising the eyebrow to make the eyes look bigger and brighter.

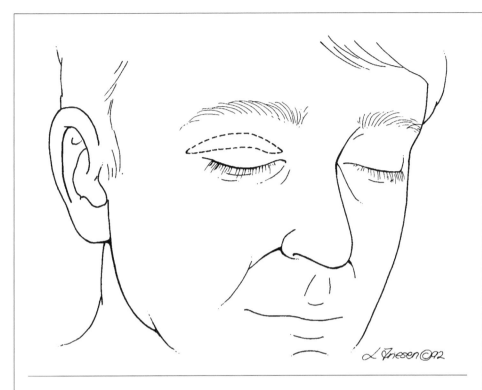

An upper blepharoplasty involves removing excess skin in the upper eyelid along with fat and a thin strip of muscle. The resulting scar is hidden in the fold of the eyelid.

are instances when an upper blepharoplasty is called for: if a patient has sagging, or draped-looking, "hooded" upper eyelids, no forehead wrinkles and the brow is resting where it should, it's an indication that the problem is limited to the eyelids and I'll go ahead with a blepharoplasty.

Another situation in which an upper blepharoplasty might be done is when a patient refuses to undergo the more extensive operation of a forehead-lift. This can be a bit frustrating for the surgeon, partly because the results won't be as good as they might have been, and partly because the forehead-lift, if the forehead is what is causing the trouble in the first place, is a more effective solution. The patient can expect a more wide-eyed, bright-eyed look after a forehead-lift.

In a piece I wrote for *The Journal of Otolaryngology*, with Dr. David K. Ward, we began with a description of the simplest upper blepharoplasty. This procedure would be suitable for a youthful patient with no droop to the forehead and only a small amount of excessive skin in the upper lid.

Once the patient has been anesthetized, a crescent-shaped segment of lid skin is cut out directly above the eye, where the resultant scar can be hidden in the natural fold. A thin strip of muscle called "orbicularis oculi" is then removed, along with any fat we might find. Often, most of the fat is found in the upper inside (medial) area of the eye and above the pupil. To close the incision, we used to have to use pull-out stitches, as opposed to stitches that needed to be snipped out. Today, we use a surgical type of Krazy Glue, sold under the brand name Histoacryl. The glue does a fine job of holding the incision shut while the skin heals, and the patient is spared the ordeal of having the stitches removed. The glue flakes off within five to seven days.

In an older patient, there will be more advanced changes in the upper lid, including increased lateral hooding and a correlating increase in what we call "redundant" orbicularis oculi, or excess muscle that contributes to sag. The solution is to take the incision out a little further toward the corner of each eye, to remove the extra muscle and skin. This results in a tiny visible scar in the skin just above the upper eyelid "sulcus," or groove. With time, however, the scar will become quite inconspicuous. A forehead-lift may also be needed.

A successful upper blepharoplasty results in a deeper, more clearly defined groove above the eye and more eyelid skin show between the groove and the eyelash line. The upper lid looks attractively sculpted. The highest compliment a surgeon can get is when people stop asking why his patient looks so tired all the time, and start commenting that his patient looks remarkably "well rested."

Fat around the eye in the upper lid is found in two distinct areas: medially, toward the inside corner of the eye and centrally, directly above the center of the eye. Fat around the eye in the lower lid is found medially, centrally and laterally — toward the

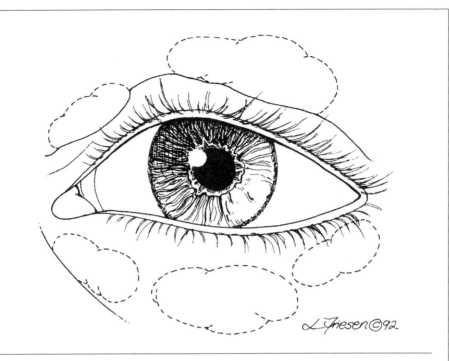

Normally, there are three fat pockets below the eye and two in the upper eyelids with no fat bulges in the upper, outer part of the eye.

outside corner of the eye. As you might recall from Chapter One on facial assessment, the way to find these pockets of fat, or fat "pads" as we call them, is to have a patient lean her head well forward in the examining room, and then look up into a mirror. This usually reveals where the skin around the eye is bulging due to excess fat.

A lower blepharoplasty operation is almost always carried out to eliminate the so-called "bags" under a patient's eyes. Sometimes it's done to get rid of coarse wrinkles, though I'd probably recommend a chemical peel for someone with no bags and only fine wrinkles or etchings, depending on whether the wrinkling was caused by too much sun, or extra skin.

In addition to the examining-room test for fat pads, a patient in need of a lower blepharoplasty must submit to the "pinch" test for laxity, or natural elasticity of the lower lid. Using my thumb and forefinger, I will lightly grasp the lower lid, pull it out a bit, then let

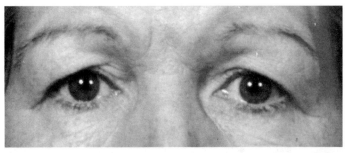

Before

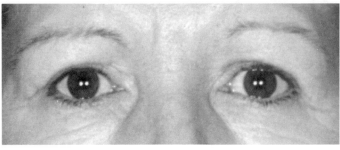

After

After an upper blepharoplasty, not only do the eyes look bigger, but the hooding of the upper lids has been removed.

go. If I can pull the lid out further than about ten millimeters, the lid lacks laxity. Similarly, if the lid fails to "snap back" into its original position, with the margin hugging the globe of the eyeball, then it lacks laxity.

We check for laxity to avoid exacerbating a phenomenon known as "scleral show" by performing a blepharoplasty. Sclera refers to the outermost layer of the three concentric layers of tissue that cover the eyeball: it is the white of the eye. Scleral show means too much of the white is showing below the iris, or colored part of the eye. You sometimes see advanced scleral show in elderly people who have lost the laxity of their lower lids. If the condition deteriorates any further, it can result in severe lower lid "ectropion," where the margin flips out and completely disengages from the eyeball. It's a look that only hound dogs should have to endure.

A patient already suffering from mild scleral show is easy to spot, but the test for laxity must be done on everyone. A patient with an

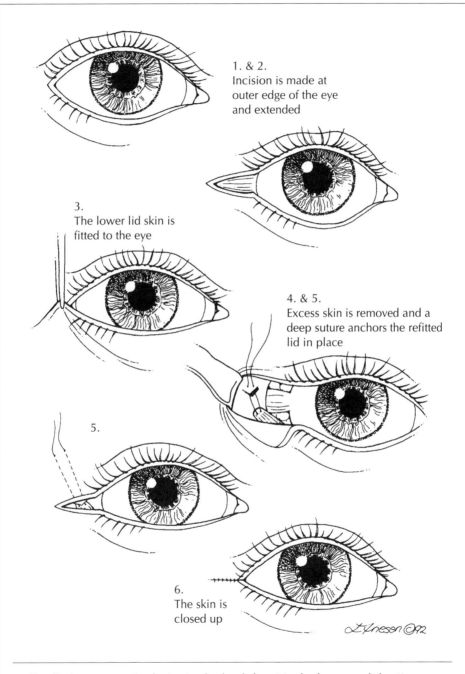

1. & 2.
Incision is made at
outer edge of the eye
and extended

3.
The lower lid skin is
fitted to the eye

4. & 5.
Excess skin is removed and a
deep suture anchors the refitted
lid in place

5.

6.
The skin is
closed up

To eliminate excessive laxity (and scleral show) in the lower eyelid, a tiny
wedge is removed from the corner of the loose lid.

undetected tendency toward scleral show might develop it after a lower blepharoplasty because the procedure removes fat and extra skin that would otherwise prop up the loose lid. Excess laxity must be surgically corrected during the blepharoplasty by tightening the lid. We can do this by cutting a tiny wedge out of the lid, at the outer corner, which shortens it horizontally. More often I'll reinforce the shortened lid with a suture that anchors it to a ligament solid to the orbital rim — the bony area surrounding the eye.

On the operating table, the search for fat pads is conducted where the incision has been made (sometimes behind the eyelid, sometimes under the lower lashes). The pads lie deep below a delicate layer of sinew called the orbital septum. The septum has the consistency of an embryonic sac, and, with age, it loses its elasticity and allows the fat pads underneath to herniate, or bulge — the way your body sometimes reveals its outline by pressing against the shower curtain. When I find the fat, it pops up slightly, distinguished by a bright yellow color.

Before snipping each fat pad away, it must first be anesthetized, because for the blepharoplasty operation, we use a local anesthetic that does not penetrate to the deep layer where the fat pads are contained in the bony orbit around the eye. So it's a matter of popping each pad, injecting it with anesthetic (usually, Xylocaine), waiting a moment for the anesthesia to take effect, snipping the pad at its root, cauterizing any tiny blood vessels bleeding into the area, and moving on to the next pad. It's a rhythmic and totally absorbing procedure that I find very satisfying, especially knowing the sometimes dramatic improvement in appearance that will follow.

The medial fat pads, those located near the inner corner of the eye, present the biggest challenge during the blepharoplasty operation. They're the hardest to find, partly because they are located furthest away from where a surgeon must stand to carry out the procedure. Remember that there usually is a surgeon accompanied by an assistant or a nurse in the operating room. The assistant is sometimes given the job of cauterizing blood vessels and the nurse

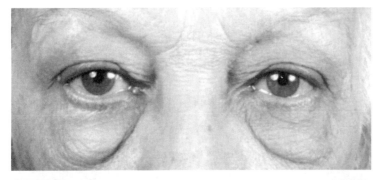
Before

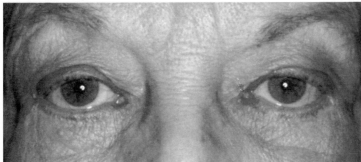
After

The result of a lower blepharoplasty is a reduction of unusually heavy bags under the eyes.

is busy monitoring a patient's reaction to anesthetic and other, intravenous fluids.

Medial fat pads can also be elusive because they're not always exactly where they're supposed to be (within millimeters, of course), or they are not as yellow as other fat pads. They tend to be whiter. But it's important that they be removed, because to leave them in would noticeably affect the overall postoperative appearance of the eye — there would be an odd pocket of fat toward the lower inner corners, made more obvious by the removal of fat centrally and laterally.

With a lower blepharoplasty, it is wise to avoid removing too much fat from the lateral compartments at the outside corner of each eye. This can result in a "hollowed" or cadaveric look if the eye globe outlines start to show. Instead of snipping out the lateral fat pads, it is sometimes wise to merely reduce them in size by cauterizing. We call this process "fat frying."

The eye region can also be affected by sagging in the forehead area; this affects the way the eyelid skin drapes over the upper eyes. Occasionally, it will even create a small hood of skin between the eyes at the top of the nose but most often it creates excessive skin at the outer, lateral edge of both eyes. Patients usually want their upper face done because their friends or coworkers have begun to remark that they look tired, or worn out. We read a lot into the face others present us with, and sometimes people with sagging foreheads are thought to be dour, or worse, dissipated.

Incision for a forehead lift

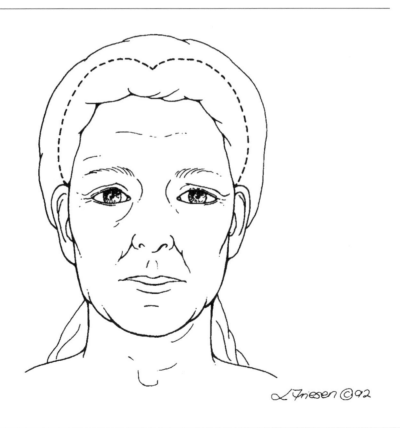

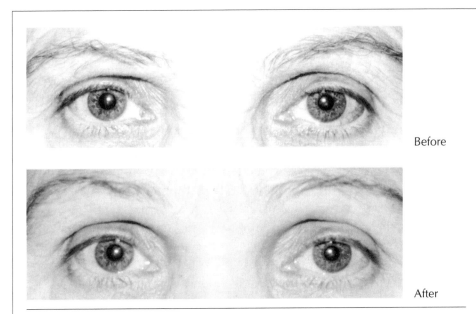

Before

After

Forehead lift: Pre-operative (above) and post-operative (below). Note the deeper upper eyelid groove in the lower picture, a result of the elevated eyebrow.

Forehead-lift

To do a forehead-lift, I make an incision in an arc roughly where a girl might wear a plastic hairband. It begins just above each ear and meets at a point at the top of the head, slightly behind the hairline to hide the long, fine scar that will result. In the case of a patient with a high forehead, the trick is to make the incision exactly along the hairline, at the junction of the hair and the forehead. This prevents the hairline from "migrating" back even further. If I am operating on a man, and he has male-pattern baldness extending well back of his scalp, the process is slightly different. I might, for example, hide the scar in an existing line on his forehead. (For more information, see Chapter Ten: Hair Transplants.)

The skin of the scalp is loosened away from the bone underneath — it actually comes away quite easily with a combination of a few scissor snips and finger manipulation — so that I can literally "pull up" the forehead to restore the position of the brows. Before pulling up, I can weaken the corrugator muscle that is responsible for deep frown lines between the eyebrows. Excess skin is cut away before closing the seam of the incision with sutures, and the operation is over, usually within an hour and a half.

As simple as it sounds, the forehead-lift is a delicate procedure because you're dealing with the big band of frontalis muscle that stretches from side to side across the forehead; the muscle that causes horizontal wrinkle lines. This muscle may have to be weakened. As well, there are the all-important frontal branches of the facial nerve that run up the sides of the face through the temple areas. These branches allow you to lift your brow into one of the many human expressions of surprise or joy or sorrow. A surgeon must be careful not to damage these nerves.

The happy result of a successful forehead-lift is that a patient's eyes look larger and brighter, primarily because they lose some of the sagging skin in the upper lid area caused by the low brow, and the eyebrows are returned to their natural position. In some cases, a patient will have come to me thinking they needed a blepharoplasty, plastic surgery of the eye, when the sagging could be corrected with a forehead-lift. However, the majority of patients need both operations.

There are a couple of other procedures related to the eye that are worth brief mention. Both are gaining in popularity, and many facial cosmetic surgeons now routinely offer these procedures as part of their service.

The Single Lid (Oriental Eye)

The first is surgery of what is known as the "Oriental" eye. Though plenty of people of Oriental extraction do, in fact, seek out the operation, it is not limited to them. The Oriental eye describes the condition in which the skin falls from the eyebrow to the upper eyelash line in a single lid. About sixty percent of Orientals have an upper lid constructed this way, and some of them don't like their appearance. The single lid can make their eyes look small and narrow. The challenge is to give them a double eyelid, with a groove between the brow and the lash line. (This is the groove where eyeshadow can be applied to give the impression of even larger, deeper-set eyes.)

Essentially, the procedure is to remove fatty tissue from the upper lid if it is excessively puffy. In order to create a groove, several sutures are used to anchor the skin to the deeper eyelid structures. I had my comeuppance on this subject when I was invited to The People's Republic of China to speak and to do some surgery and I had prepared a talk on the Oriental eye procedure. By then, I'd handled about fifty-five such operations. The organizers of the symposium were terribly polite about it, but they did tell me that they'd collectively handled about 10,000 cases themselves. I spoke on a different topic.

Permanent Lash Enhancement

A second popular procedure concerning the eye is permanent eyelash enhancement. Eyelash enhancement is a fancy term for medical tattooing. It takes about an hour, and it has to be done under a special magnifying loop. All sorts of people find it an appealing procedure, including women who are too busy to bother with makeup, women who have physical trouble applying makeup due to arthritis or poor vision, men (especially those in the entertainment business) who don't want to apply makeup, allergy sufferers, contact lens wearers, people with oily skin whose makeup tends to smear or fade, athletes who want to look good during and after exercise and, of course, the woman who refuses to be seen without makeup.

In some ways, the procedure reminds me of the way people used to write with quill pens: the method is to dip the needle into a small vial of dye, then apply the dye in a series of tiny dots along the lash line, between and around the existing lashes. The needle is equipped with a reciprocating motor, so the dots can be made quickly and with precision. When you see the dots from a distance, they give the appearance of eyeliner around the eye, but seen under a magnifying loop, they are revealed as a mosaic. As you can imagine, it's important to select exactly the right pigment to complement a patient's hair, eye coloring and skin tone. Permanent eyelash enhancement will look completely natural when successfully done, even in the case of an albino patient with the palest of lashes or an accident victim with no eyelashes, or sparse eyelashes.

The amount of pigment used is minimal, as it is considered a base type of eyeliner. At night, patients can still put on their high-fashion makeup. Eyelash framing, as this procedure is sometimes called, can be traced through history from ancient Egyptian times through the Middle Ages to the present day.

Before undergoing permanent lash enhancement, it is wise to make sure you have no infections of the eye or temporary allergy symptoms. It's also a good idea to stop wearing makeup a couple of days before the operation, and for at least a week afterward. The procedure can be done under a light local anesthetic, and you'll be given an ointment to apply afterward each night to aid healing. Makeup and the use of contact lenses can be resumed once the ointment has removed the crust and there is no danger of infection.

As often happens with cosmetic surgery, there are other uses that have been refined as a result of technical progress. Medical tattooing, for example, can also be used to treat "white spots," the patches that show a loss of pigmentation, often on the back of an elderly patient's hands. With properly selected and blended dyes, the patches can be made to match perfectly with the surrounding skin.

One other use of medical tattooing has proved less than successful, however. Though it would seem to be a logical use of the procedure, tattooing to produce a permanent lip liner is a little risky. A lot of people have a serious allergic reaction to the reddish-colored dyes, which contain iron oxide.

Aside from scleral show or ectropion, the most serious complication that can arise after blepharoplasty is blindness, though such a possibility is extremely rare. If an incised fat pad starts to bleed into the orbit behind the eye, it could cause compression and a loss of blood supply to the eye, resulting in blindness. This is thought to happen when a patient has premature hardening of the eye arteries and these fine little arteries open up and start to bleed. Before a patient undergoes blepharoplasty, I strongly advise a visit to an ophthalmologist, who will check the back of each eye for potential problems.

Another complication might be asymmetry, when a blepharoplasty makes one eye slightly different in shape to the other. In most cases, this is not a serious problem, as few people in the world are born with perfectly symmetrical eyes to begin with. In fact, they are not identical on either side of an imaginary, central line; they are asymmetrical. But obviously there is a tolerable degree of asymmetry, and this can usually be achieved by taking precautionary steps before the operation.

I have my patients sit up straight on the operating table while I outline with a felt pen exactly where the offending fat pads are, and where I intend to cut. Once the patient is lying down, the fat pads often disappear, so the pen lines serve as an important guide once the operation is underway. (I use this same method to give myself a blueprint for most of the operations I do. It wouldn't be wise to ask a patient to sit up halfway through a procedure just so I could remember the distribution of facial features before we started.)

And finally, a complication might arise from blepharoplasty if a surgeon removes too much upper eyelid skin and the patient is unable to properly close the eye. Blinking enables us to disperse the natural liquid that forms a film over the eyeball. If it's a particularly bad case, the patient might suffer from "dry eye" when the eyeball dries from constant exposure to the air without blinking. Some patients have a natural dry eye tendency which should be assessed before surgery. The operation to correct this problem involves grafting skin from a site behind the ear onto the too-short eyelid to give it back its proper length and the use of eyedrops and ointment to keep the eye lubricated.

All of the complications I've mentioned — scleral show, ectropion, asymmetry, dry eye, tearing and blindness — are rare occurrences. Perhaps one percent of patients might be susceptible to developing complications to varying degrees, and even this low number depends on the individual patient's health to begin with. Blindness, especially, is a comfortably remote possibility. But it's important that you know how delicate a procedure blepharoplasty is. Make sure you are completely confident in your surgeon and don't be afraid to ask for references from one of the professional associations.

CHAPTER FOUR

Acne Scarring

TEENAGERS ARE SURELY AMONG the bravest souls on earth, heading into the responsibilities of adulthood even while their bodies work to betray them. Puberty brings with it an increase in male hormones in both girls and boys, which causes all manner of disruption — especially at high school dances — but the worst of it, any teenager will tell you, is acne.

Acne vulgaris is the medical term for the kind of acne that plagues most teenagers. The word *vulgaris*, by the way, is the Latin word for "common": it is the most common kind of acne. There are other kinds of acne, like *acne rosacea*, but *acne vulgaris* is the kind that, at its worst, causes scarring in about five percent of the kids who are afflicted with it.

Acne vulgaris is a chronic inflammatory disease of the "pilosebaceous follicles" of the skin. As mentioned in the chapter on aging skin (Chapter Two), skin is composed of two layers: the thin upper layer called the epidermis, and a thicker layer below called the dermis. Below the skin is the subcutaneous layer of mostly fatty tissue surrounding essential blood vessels. The "follicles" are small sacs in the dermis layer, each with a canal leading to the surface of the skin. "Pilosebaceous" refers to a unit consisting of a hair follicle, a fine shaft of hair and a sebaceous gland.

Male hormones stimulate the sebaceous glands to increase production of the oily substance known as sebum. Ordinarily, and in the

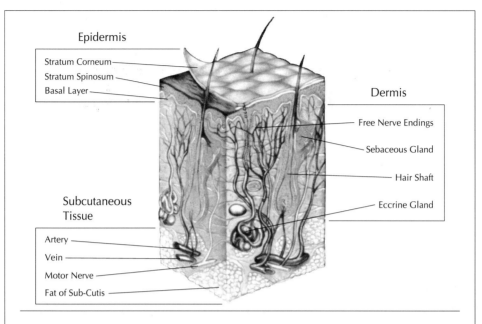

Epidermis

Stratum Corneum
Stratum Spinosum
Basal Layer

Dermis

Free Nerve Endings

Sebaceous Gland

Hair Shaft

Eccrine Gland

Subcutaneous
Tissue

Artery
Vein
Motor Nerve
Fat of Sub-Cutis

Detail of skin

right amounts, sebum is a friendly substance that acts to keep the hair and skin lubricated and supple, with a moisturized appearance. But some teenagers produce too much sebum during the years of hormonal imbalance, and this is where the trouble starts.

As it always does, the basal or bottom layer of the epidermis goes about the business of manufacturing new skin cells. Usually, these cells migrate with sebum to the surface of the skin through the follicular canals mentioned above. This regenerative process slows down with age, but teenagers actually produce a brand new "stratum corneum," or outer layer of skin, every fourteen days.

(The stratum corneum, also known as keratin, is the top of five thin layers that make up the epidermis. In descending order, the remaining four layers are the stratum lucidum, stratum granulosum, stratum spinosum and stratum basale.)

As the sebum and new cells work their way up to the surface, they can become blocked, especially in the skin of teenagers. This is because the follicular canals are stopped up with an excessive amount of sebum, which is very sticky. The problem gets worse when skin cells unable to

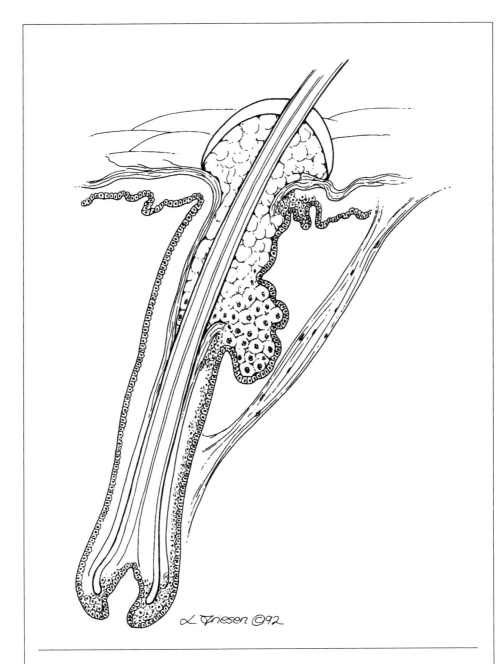

Sebum and new cells can become trapped in the follicular canal as they work their way to the surface of the skin. The blockage results in whiteheads that can lead to pimples or acne.

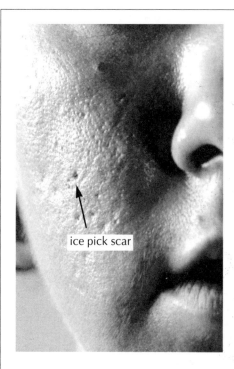
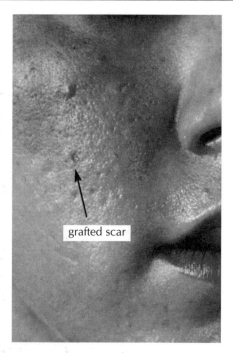

ice pick scar

grafted scar

Deep ice pick scars can be disguised with dermal punch grafting or excision.

reach the surface die and begin to accumulate in the passageway. This build-up of dead skin cells results in a plug called a comedo.

The traffic jam in the follicular canals I've just described leads to mere pimples in most teenagers. But in some, an extra factor is at work: a bacteria called P. Acnes. In the unfortunate five percent who go on to develop *acne vulgaris*, the Propionibacterium Acnes (P. Acnes, for short) bacteria in their system causes inflammation.

The sequence of events is: male hormones stimulate extra production of sebum, which plugs the follicular canals; the problem is made worse by a build-up of keratin and a comedo is created; the comedo finally grows so big that it ruptures through the follicular canals and the sticky keratin seeps out into the dermis; and there, the P. Acnes bacteria causes infection, and the infection causes inflammation. The body's answer to inflammation below the skin is a scar.

Types of Scars

The kind of scars caused by acne usually are "nonlinear," meaning they do not have length. People who have been in a car accident, or suffered wounding from a knife, for example, would have long linear scars to deal with. Instead, a typical nonlinear scar caused by acne looks like a small pit in the surface of the skin. A more dramatic kind of scar caused by acne is the "ice pick" scar. This is a tiny, but very deep, pit in the surface of the skin — it looks like someone has taken an ice pick to the skin and punched a hole.

The body repairs itself by forming scars. After the infection and the inflammation caused by P. Acnes has subsided, the body repairs the damage done by creating a scar. It's a process that might be repeated again and again over several years. The extent of and nature of scarring will depend on the depth and intensity of damage, and the length of time an area suffered inflammation. The result is an "underground," or subcutaneous, network of scars: individual pits that show on the surface and tunnels that connect some of them below. Tunneling happens when two or more follicular canals rupture at the same time and join together as they heal.

Wide dermal scars can be treated successfully with dermabrasion and/or injections.

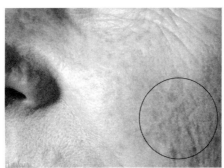

Before

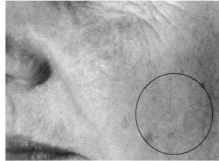

After

To describe the condition to my patients, I sometimes use the layout of a bungalow for illustration. Think of the hallway in the bungalow as the tunneling. The hallway leads into various rooms, some of which have exits to the outdoors, some of which don't. The rooms with exits are like fistulas in the skin that show on the surface with pits. The rooms without exits are cysts: pockets created under the skin attached to one another with tunnels, but with no exit to the surface. The scarring that you see on the surface might not reveal the full extent of scarring beneath the skin, just as a bungalow with a front and a back door doesn't reveal all its rooms. And so, inflammation caused by acne creates tunnels, fistulas and cysts. The entire microscopic network is rigidly cast with scarring.

The first thing I'll do when a patient comes to me with acne scarring is examine the scars under an overhead light. Most acne scars are pits less than five millimeters in diameter with sharp "shoulders" perpendicular to the skin. They aren't much wider than this because the hair follicle itself is only one or two millimeters in diameter, so the subsequent scar created in the follicular canal is not significantly bigger. Acne scars vary in size and shape from being relatively shallow to being narrow and very deep — the ice pick scars. As most public places are lit from above, it's important to see how light is catching the scars. The rough edges of the pits actually cast tiny dark shadows.

Underneath the surface of the skin, subcutaneous scarring can cause a second visual effect by altering the contours of the face. Scarring causes a certain loss of tissue under the dermis layer of skin, and if the scarring extends over a wide-enough area, it'll create a noticeable depression, a kind of shallow crater like you see on the surface of the moon. We call these "flat ovoid depressions"; they can be as wide as two centimeters in diameter.

Another kind of subcutaneous scarring results in "undulations," or a washboard effect, especially in the cheek area. When scars mature, they contract, and if the scarring beneath the skin is extensive enough, the skin will pull up like an accordian under the surface.

Most acne patients have a combination of the various effects of scarring, though one kind of scarring often dominates. And the combination might vary from one area of the face to another. The center of a cheek might show mostly ice pick scars; toward the outside edges of the cheek, the scarring might be wider and shallower. The chin sometimes produces its own sort of scarring, called nodular scarring, which shows up as a patch of tiny bumps. The bumps are permanent scars that have thickened with age.

The thing about any kind of scarring, acne scarring included, is that a facial cosmetic surgeon can rarely take it away, or get rid of it. What we can do, as noted earlier, is play tricks with the eye so that the scarring is camouflaged. It's a kind of *trompe-l'oeil* where we alter the scarring so that light reflects on it differently or so that it fits the contours of the face in a subtler way.

Before anything can be done for a patient with acne scarring, the acne itself has to be permanently quiescent, meaning no longer active or continuing to produce eruptions. For most people, the worst of it is over by their mid-twenties, and we can start to treat them, but there is a relatively new drug on the market that helps to quiet the acne more quickly. It is 13-cis-retinoic acid — called Accutane.

Accutane was developed by the Roche drug company about six or seven years ago. It is available by prescription through dermatologists. What it does is slow down the maturation process of the epidermis, when, as I explained earlier, the cells migrate up from the basal layer to the surface to create new skin. Accutane "normalizes" the process in teens who are producing too much sebum and too much keratin. They stop having the problems of inflammation caused by plugged follicular canals.

Accutane is a very powerful drug, and the *Compendium of Pharmaceuticals and Specialties* lists many possible side effects. For example, Accutane is considered very dangerous to a fetus — no pregnant woman should consider taking it. Patients usually take it in cycles of only three or four months at a time, sometimes extended over a couple of years. It was originally prescribed by dermatologists for extremely bad cases of cystic acne. Now, with careful supervision and monitoring, including monthly liver tests, they'll use it on less active forms of *acne vulgaris.*

I can't do much for patients with acne scarring until the acne is quiescent and/or they've been off Accutane for at least six months.

This is because some of the effects of the drug are still at work on the epidermis, slowing down the creation of new skin. But the procedures we use to treat acne scarring require plenty of healing, and healing is partly a function of generating new skin.

Scar Treatments

There are five methods for improving the scarring left behind by *acne vulgaris:* dermabrasion; injectable substances; dermal punch grafting; excision; and face-lifting.

Dermabrasion

Dermabrasion, or dermal leveling, is what we call the "workhorse" technique. It involves planing the normal, unaffected skin surrounding the scar pits so that the skin is thinned to the level of the bottom of the pit — or as close to the bottom as we can get. In other words, if you dug a hole in your garden and wanted to make the hole less obvious, you could either fill it up to bring it level with the surrounding earth, or you could dig away at the earth surrounding the hole until it ceased to exist because the surrounding surface had become level with the bottom of the hole. Dermabrasion makes the scar pits so shallow that they appear to be more level with the surrounding, normal skin.

What we are doing is actually removing the top layer of skin, the epidermis, and planing down into the dermis layer. As the patient heals from the operation, new skin cells push up to the surface to create a new epidermis. Most patients with acne scarring who have undergone dermabrasion heal in about seven days, but the maturing process takes a little longer. This means that the epidermis has healed after a week or so, but the skin is still red in color because the keratin layer has not yet been restored to its normal thickness. The good news is that no skin on the body regenerates faster than facial skin: it is extremely rich in pilosebaceous units. You could never, for example, dermabrade the skin on the inside of a patient's arm. It wouldn't regenerate quickly enough or in a great-enough quantity to prevent scarring from the process itself.

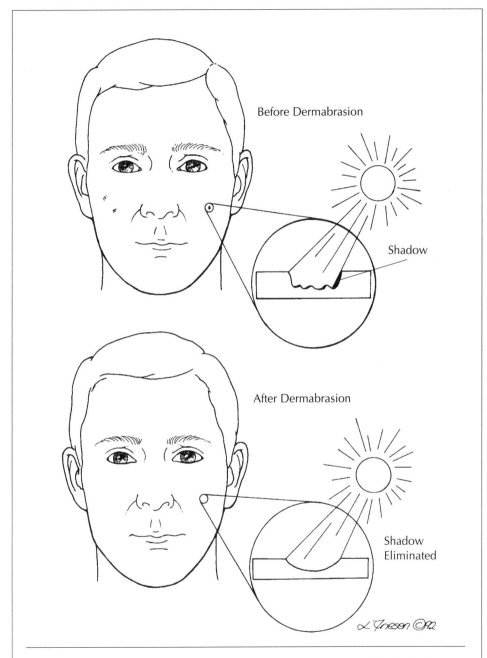

Before Dermabrasion

Shadow

After Dermabrasion

Shadow
Eliminated

The skin before and after dermabrasion. The shadowing caused by light playing on the deep pits is eliminated once the skin has been thinned and the pits have been made more saucer-like.

The process of dermabrasion can be used to improve the appearance of acne scarring and superficial scarring caused by accident, as well as freckles, some birthmarks and tattoos. Patients can be dermabraded under general anesthesia or under local anesthesia in a condition of conscious sedation. The skin can then be "frozen" with an anesthetic skin refrigerant called Fridgaderm. Dermabrasion is a vigorous action, and the skin must be taut or "frozen" to be worked on. Freezing keeps the bleeding to a minimum during the procedure.

According to a text on the subject, by Dr. E. Gaylon McCollough and Dr. Phillip Royal Langsdon, published by Thieme Medical Publishers in New York, carpenter sandpaper was originally used to hand-plane the skin. Then the idea of a motor-driven instrument was developed, and some surgeons tried hooking up a dental drill to sandpaper discs. Today, like me, most surgeons prefer the modern electrical units, available with a variety of tips appropriate to the task at hand, such as wire brushes, diamond fraises and serrated, stainless-steel wheels. I prefer to use the diamond fraise, which is a round metal cylinder with diamond chips on it. Whichever implement is used, however, there's no getting around the fact it's a bit of a messy job that requires a steady hand.

Dermabrasion is ideally suited to patients with wide, shallow pits in the skin. This is not a procedure for ice pick scars. The idea is to round the shoulders of the pit so that there is less shadowing at the bottom of the pit. Obviously, the less severe the problem is before we start, the more effective dermabrasion will be: it isn't safe to go too deeply through the dermis as this action itself will cause scarring. Occasionally, I'll treat a patient with dermabrasion twice over the course of several years, which allows for healing periods of more than twelve months.

Generally speaking, it's a good idea to dermabrade an entire regional aesthetic unit of the face at one time. By this, I mean doing the entire forehead, or an entire cheek, even if only part of the area is affected. This is because dermabrasion affects the skin's pigmentation by making it lighter in color. The trick is to go a bit deeper in the area that needs dermabrasion, then to "feather" lightly toward the edges so that the aesthetic unit blends nicely with the rest of the face.

Many surgeons refuse to dermabrade people of Negroid or Oriental extraction because dermabrasion can make the affected areas patchy and lighter in color. But it's been my experience that the lightened areas darken with healing and that the overall effect can be quite acceptable over a period of time in some patients. As well, I usually do a test area behind the ear to determine the degree of discoloration. If the patient is willing to accept patchy, discolored skin for up to a year after the operation, I see no reason to deny it. However, I don't like to dermabrade Caucasian people with olive-colored skin. The dermabrasion seems to leave permanent brown and lighter colored blotches. To my eye, the blotches are usually more noticeable than the original problem of acne scarring, so it doesn't make any sense.

Within eighteen to twenty-four hours after dermabrasion, the regeneration of skin begins. There are two ways to handle the healing process that follows dermabrasion: let a crust form (basically, a giant scab on the face) that will shed in about seven to twelve days, or keep the surface of the face moist. To keep the skin moist, Polysporin ointment, mineral oil or Crisco shortening can be applied. Most of my patients prefer the ointment because it is less messy than the other two lubricants. However I favor the covered approach using some of the new "breathing" or moist dressings: studies have shown that regeneration is speeded up with a dressing. These days I use a spray sealant called Tisseel as well.

Once the dressing comes off, in about five to seven days, the dermabraded skin will be very red at the beginning, then fade to lessening degrees of pink over the next eight weeks. It's very important to completely avoid the sun and then to wear a broad spectrum sunscreen with an SPF (sun protection factor) of at least 15 for the next six months. Otherwise, the bright pink patches might become permanently brown.

As with the chemical peel process I described earlier, dermabrasion is likely to cause some swelling, especially if it's been done around the eyes or lips. The swelling will be most obvious by the end of the second day after the operation, and then it begins to subside. It helps to sleep with your head propped up by a couple of pillows at night; elevation seems to bring the swelling down a little faster as the swelling is gravity-dependent.

Also similar to the chemical peel process is the warning not to pick away any adherent crust that forms on the skin. This could damage the dermis layer and cause infection and scarring. And, as with chemical peel, about thirty percent of patients will experience some form of depression. The depression is at least partly attributable to the psychological impact of seeing your face in the early postoperative period: it'll be messy. If it happens to you, just try to remember that it is a perfectly normal reaction and that the feeling will pass.

Several weeks or months after dermabrasion is done, some patients might experience the appearance of "milia" on the skin. These are tiny white bumps, named for their resemblance to millet seeds. They are caused by keratin plugging the sweat glands — some people, in fact, develop milia as a reaction to prickly heat. Usually, the condition disappears on its own, but if it persists, the bumps can be uncapped with a needle by your surgeon and made to disperse. In any case, milia is nothing to worry about.

Most patients can return to work or a reasonably active social life about two weeks after dermabrasion with makeup applied by an aes-

Nodular scarring

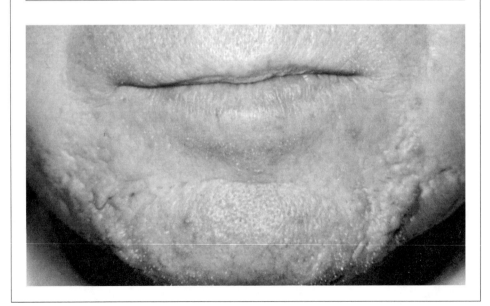

thetician or a camouflage makeup specialist. The redness and some splotchy patches will persist a while longer, but water-based makeup will conceal the worst of it. Very occasionally, a patient will develop fever blisters during these first weeks, and medication can be prescribed to settle them down. Patients who've had dermabrasion done on the nose should avoid wearing eyeglasses for at least two weeks after, so this could affect the speed with which normal life is resumed. And, a final word of advice, athletically inclined patients shouldn't exercise strenuously for at least a month following the procedure. Extreme changes in temperature or flushing will exacerbate the redness on a temporary basis. The new skin you are growing is as delicate as a newborn baby's. Remember to keep ultraviolet rays off your face and wear your sun bonnet!

I mentioned earlier an unusual kind of scarring caused by acne that sometimes appears on the chin: nodular scarring. These tiny bumps, measuring three to five millimeters in diameter, do not respond well to dermabrasion. It is better to apply "electrical hyfrecation," and the results are usually good. A "hyfrecator" looks something like a ballpoint pen casing, with a fine needle at one end. It is attached to a machine that emits radio waves, or electric currents, to actually "fry away" each nodular scar.

My experience has been that it is better to hyfrecate the chin over two or more sessions, doing only a small section at a time. For some reason, when the entire chin is hyfrecated, the patient can end up with what we call an "exuberant" healing process, and the end result isn't nearly as level. Actually, exuberant healing from the inflammation of acne is exactly what caused the thickened nodular scars in the first place. So, nodular scarring is best treated in several short sessions.

Injections

The use of injectable substances is the second method of treatment for scarring left behind by acne. There are two kinds of substances commonly used: triamcinolone acetonide, known as Kenalog and a collagen implant called Zyplast. The Kenalog injection is a corti-

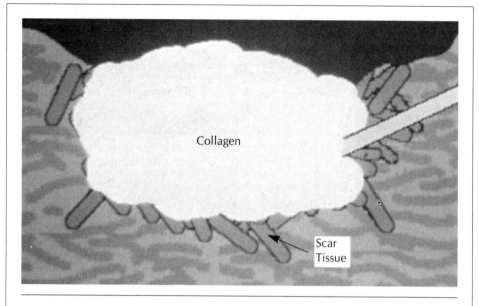

An injectable filler like collagen can be used to smooth out depressed scars to make the surface of the skin level.

sone shot — a steroid. It works to dissolve solid scars, or what we call fibrocytes. Kenalog is a catabolic substance, meaning it interacts with the scar to break it down. A surgeon has to read the situation carefully before using Kenalog as it can be used in higher or lower strengths (for example, ten to forty milligrams per cc). The higher potency sometimes acts too efficiently and begins to break down the scar tissue too fast, so that you end up with a slight depression where the scar has collapsed. Kenalog is particularly effective when used on bumps or nodules caused by inflammation.

The second kind of injectable substance, the collagen implant called Zyplast, is a three-dimensional volume filler, meaning it will fill the width, depth and height of a hole in the skin. For more information on collagen, see the chapter on aging skin (Chapter Two). The idea is to fill a hole, or pit, so that the bottom of the pit is raised to become level with the surrounding skin. The most successful injections are those done in pits located in "nondynamic" areas of the face, that is, parts of the face that don't move much. The injection wouldn't last nearly as long in a pit located in a frown line or a laugh line; it might last as long as six months at the outside edge of a cheek or on the chin. As I explained earlier, collagen is a biodegradable product, so it's not a permanent solution. Nevertheless it results in a spectacular smoothing of the skin surface.

Even though it would seem the perfect solution, Zyplast does not work when applied to the ice pick scar. This is partly because an ice pick scar — being very deep and narrow — cannot be made less conspicuous by raising the depth of the scar or narrowing the opening at the surface. Often, too, an ice pick scar is very compacted, with more rigid walls than an ordinary acne pit. This means that the scar doesn't yield at all when injected, and the Zyplast gets forced up through the centre of the pit.

Zyplast is best used on flat, shallow acne pits and areas where there is subcutaneous atrophy (a wasting away of fat under the skin). I often use it to temporarily augment surgical techniques like dermabrasion or dermal punch grafting. It's a nice technique, for example, if a patient wants to look as good as possible for a photo portrait, or a wedding day.

Dermal Punch Grafting

Dermal punch grafting, the third technique in a surgeon's arsenal against the effects of acne scarring, is ideal for some ice pick scars. The "punch" is a tiny round cylinder, and it comes in a variety of sizes up to about five millimeters in diameter. The cylinder has a wickedly sharp edge at the bottom, just like a razor, and I apply this edge to the skin while rotating the cylinder between my thumb and forefinger. The cylinder punches through the surface of the skin and bores through the dermis to neatly cut out the scar tissue in a kind of core drilling exercise. (Hair transplants are punched out using the same technique, though a surgeon will usually resort to a motor-driven attachment if he's doing a lot of grafts at once.)

Once the punch has been made, the skin graft to be applied to the site is "harvested" from behind the ear. The skin high on the bone behind the ear is ideal for grafts because it is one of the few places on the human body that doesn't grow any hair. (You don't want great long hairs sprouting from your face, especially if you're a woman.) This skin also presents a good color match (but not perfect) with facial skin. Generally speaking, dermal punch grafting is used on scars, ice pick and otherwise, with a diameter of between three and five millimeters. If an ice pick scar is smaller, say two millimeters wide, I might just take a stitch and close up the hole without bothering to graft. Otherwise, Histoacryl is applied to the graft; we no longer have to bother with sutures.

Sometimes, grafting becomes a two-stage procedure: the graft heals into a tiny bump slightly higher that the surrounding skin; this bump is then removed with a more general dermabrasion procedure. The two-stage approach is taken over a six-month or year-long period of time, to allow for complete healing before deciding whether the dermabrasion is necessary.

Patients with acne scarring so severe that it requires grafting are often slow to heal from the grafts. This is because they have such trou-

A line formed by a series of deep dermal scars can be minimized by scar excision. The scars are cut out and replaced with a single scar that runs parallel to the relaxed skin tension lines (wrinkles).

Before

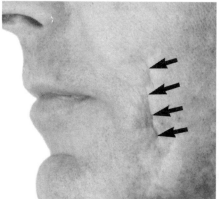

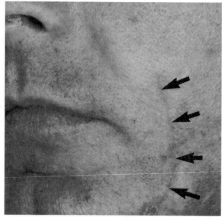

After

bled skin to begin with: the oiliness, or sebaceousness, means that the composition of their skin makes it more prone to infection. As a result, we often must prescribe tetracycline or minocycline — antibiotics — for a period of time to help decrease the bacteria, P. Acnes, that is causing and recausing infection. Some patients are allergic to such medication, so their ability to heal from grafting might be limited.

If the patient's skin shows pit-type scars greater in circumference than five millimeters, it is still possible to try grafting, but it might result in a shallow depression when the graft heals. Overall, this produces what we call a "cobblestone" effect, especially if there have been several such grafts — the skin looks faintly like the surface of a cobblestone driveway. If this occurs, the condition can be improved with dermabrasion, or even collagen injections. But usually, it is unnecessary.

Excision

Excision, the fourth method of treating acne scarring, involves excising or cutting out a series of old acne scars and replacing them with a single linear scar. Sometimes the old scars have produced tunneling, where two or more pits have joined beneath the skin. The most dramatic case of tunneling I've ever seen was when we started examining a patient's acne-scarred nose and the pits extended from the top of the nose down its length to a spot just above the nasal tip. It looked like a honeycomb when we lifted off the skin to reveal the tunneling.

No matter what the cause of such scarring, it does not respond as well to grafting as it does to excision. We simply go in there and cut out the scar and then sew it up, just like an ordinary wound. Unlike with most other acne scarring techniques, Histoacryl glue is not enough to hold the wound together, so slowly absorbing sutures placed under the skin are used instead. These are stitches that will eventually disappear in the body so they don't have to be removed. We sew on two levels: a deep dermal stitch anchors the wound together from below; surface sutures keep it as level as possible.

The cosmetic trick behind excision is to hide the new scar in an existing wrinkle or at the junction of two regional aesthetic units like the lip and the cheek. Near the beginning of this chapter, I mentioned that plastic surgery applied to acne scarring is the art of *trompe-l'oeil*, or tricking the eye. Acne scarring is nonlinear scarring, which is why it's so noticeable on the face. With excision, we replace it with linear scarring and fold it into the existing lines of the face. The eye is fooled — though there are still scars, they are different and less obvious.

Any patient who undergoes excision should try to remember the "six and six" rule: at six weeks, the new scars will look their worst; at six months, the scars start to mature. At six weeks, the body is working furiously to lay down natural collagen and pump blood to the scars so that they will heal. As a result, this is when scars are bright red. Slowly, over the next couple of months, the scars will turn lighter and lighter shades of pink. Then, six months after the operation (I've seen it happen nearly to the day), the scars begin to whiten. A mature scar is a white scar. If properly concealed, it will be barely noticeable.

Face-lift

The fifth, and final, way of treating acne scarring is to perform a face-lift. Twenty years ago, when I started in my career, this was the only technique at hand for dealing with the undulation or "washboard" effect of excessive scarring deep in the skin. The trouble is, it's a temporary sort of solution because all that a face-lift can effect in this instance is a "stretching" of the subcutaneous scar in an effort to camouflage the rippling below. It's a bit like making the bed without bothering to smooth the bottom sheets first: the creases will show through once all the covers are settled into place.

Today, facial cosmetic surgeons will work on this sort of acne scarring by changing the appearance of the rippling or depressions in the skin by simply injecting three-dimensional volume fillers, such as collagen. Whatever the approach, the past two decades have advanced our ability to treat acne scarring to the extent that the face-lift is now rarely used as a technique.

CHAPTER FIVE

Accidents

SAD TO SAY, accidents, especially motor vehicle accidents, provide most facial cosmetic surgeons with a steady stream of customers. Many years ago, I did some research and prepared a paper for a medical publication on the subject of facial injuries. It was ground-breaking news at the time, but I found a direct link between the number of patients I saw with severe facial fractures and those who confessed that they were not using a seat belt at the time of the accident.

An insurance company picked up on the story, and on January 1, 1976, the Province of Ontario became the first major North American jurisdiction to enact legislation for the compulsory use of seat-belt restraints. Concurrent legislation was enacted to reduce highway speed limits. My earlier research focused primarily on bony injuries; with Dr. John D. Keohane, I have since done further research into soft tissue injuries, and in February 1991 we published a paper on trauma assessment and scar revision.

I am pleased to say that nowadays we see fewer patients with injuries from windshields and the like. But accidents do happen, and this chapter is about the sorts of things that we do to repair such injuries, with special emphasis on the techniques we use to repair soft tissue or facial skin scars.

Most wounds inflicted on facial soft tissues are minor; and they heal quickly without much lasting effect. This is partly because the face regenerates skin faster than anyplace else on the body. It's also because the face is blessed with a rich supply of oxygen-bearing blood from two major arteries located on either side of the head; we call them the internal and external carotid arteries.

The internal carotid artery supplies blood to the brain and its coverings, as well as the eye and its orbital contents. But the primary supply of blood comes from the external artery, which is connected to a network that feeds the face, neck and scalp. Both the internal and external arteries have hundreds of tiny capillary connections so that facial wounds are likely to bleed more vigorously than cuts to other parts of the body. The bounty of blood also means that the chances of having a facial wound become infected are considerably lower than the chances of infection in wounds anywhere else.

Emergency Care

When an accident victim with facial wounding arrives through the emergency door at a hospital, emergency officers do the ABCs of assessing and stabilizing the victim's injuries before a facial cosmetic surgeon is called to the scene. (The ABCs of trauma are: airway, breathing and circulation.) These doctors have to make sure the patient has a clear airway to the lungs, that he is breathing properly and that his blood pressure is maintaining circulation. Checking for nerve damage is the next step. Where facial nerves are concerned, an otolaryngologist — a head and neck surgeon like myself — is called in.

Different nerves control sensory and motor functions of the face. Sensory functions, like the ability to feel cold, heat or pain, are controlled by branches of the trigeminal nerve. (Part of this nerve also animates the muscles used for chewing.) Motor functions, such as lifting eyebrows or smiling, are controlled by the facial nerve.

The trigeminal and facial nerves are two of the twelve cranial nerves, nerves that grow from the brain stem to the peripheral areas of the head. There are several tests that reveal if these nerves have been damaged, including a simple visual inspection. If wounding is deep in the cheek area or in the glandular area near the base of each ear, it is possible that the facial nerve has been damaged. Or, if the patient shows areas of "hypoesthesia" in the cheeks — insensitivity to pain — a branch of the trigeminal nerve might be ruptured due to a fracture in the eye socket.

Emergency doctors check, too, for any indication of facial paralysis, which would indicate nerve damage. Similarly, if there are broken bones, or other kinds of related injuries, these must be addressed by specialists before any work can begin on repair of the soft tissues of the face.

If a wound is contaminated with foreign objects like dirt or glass, it has to be cleaned out, or irrigated. Three-percent hydrogen peroxide, straight from the bottle, is an ideal wound irrigator as it tends to foam away any debris and remove blood staining at the same time. This makes it easier to see more clearly into the wound. Depending on how the wound was caused, doctors might have to administer antibiotics at this stage; dog bites and human bites, for example, almost always justify the use of antibiotics to be on the safe side against possible infection.

After a patient has been stabilized with cleansing and anesthesia, the next task is to preserve all living tissue in the wounded areas and to surgically remove all dead tissue. Of course, because of the copious amount of bleeding in facial wounds, the wounds may have to be cauterized as the doctors proceed. The process of cauterization involves singeing the open ends of blood vessels, one at a time, with an electric current, so that they stop bleeding. Once all the wounds and injuries are assessed, a treatment plan can be started. The emergency doctor might refer the more complex facial injuries to appropriate specialists — like, among others, a facial cosmetic surgeon.

Minimizing Scarring

Before deciding on the cosmetic repair procedures, we'll make an assessment of the kind of wounding we are looking at. Some wounds are jagged tears called lacerations. Some are scrapes, or abrasions. Often, wounding by accident is a combination of lacerations and abrasions. There might also be puncture wounds or avulsions, where a part of the face has been torn away. Accidental wounding usually results in a number of contusions as well, otherwise known as bruises.

With each kind of wounding, it is important to measure the length and depth of the wound, and its location within or crossing regional aesthetic units. I've mentioned before that the eight regional aesthetic units of the face are the scalp, forehead, eyes, cheeks, lips (combined with the area surrounding the mouth), nose, chin, and neck. We look to see the direction a wound takes through a regional aesthetic unit and whether a tear in the skin is within what we call a "relaxed skin tension line."

Each of the regional aesthetic units has its own set of relaxed skin tension lines — more commonly referred to as wrinkles. Sometimes we call these particular wrinkles "facial dynamic lines" because they correspond to underlying muscles that create movement in the face. In each region, the relaxed skin tension lines, or wrinkles, run perpendicular to the direction of muscle pull. The forehead muscle, for example, pulls vertically hence, the forehead wrinkles are horizontal. The wrinkle at the outside juncture of the cheek and lip regions is vertically curved. This is because the smiling muscles pull upward and outward.

Facial dynamic or relaxed skin tension lines.

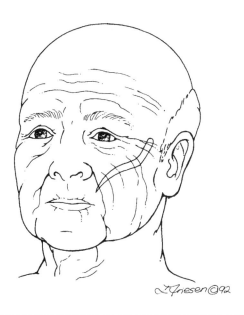

L. Friesen ©92

A scar crossing two or more aesthetic units can be hidden in the facial dynamic lines

There are a couple of reasons for checking to see if a laceration lies within one of these relaxed skin tension lines. For one, if it does, the laceration will generally heal in a more cosmetically pleasing way than it might otherwise. For another, wounding hidden within these lines is likely to heal in a barely noticeable scar, so it might not need much cosmetic surgery.

If a wound extends across two or more regional aesthetic units, it will create the kind of facial scarring that may be psychologically upsetting. First impressions make lasting impressions, and our society reserves harsh judgment for people afflicted with noticeable facial scars. Often, we impute an unsavory character to someone known as "scarface." The magic of the cosmetic surgeon is to be able to camouflage a scar so that it folds naturally into the hiding places of the face: the relaxed skin tension lines.

Generally speaking, the face is an ideal place to perform cosmetic surgery because most of its skin can be manipulated easily; facial skin is mobile. This is true of all but the skin at the base of the nose and the corners of each eye, which is why, for example, a patient might end up with a scar that "pulls" on the eye if it extends into one of the more mobile regions.

If we are involved during the stages immediately after an accident, before we can start to fine-tune the transition from wounding to camouflaged scarring, we have to deal with closing up the torn skin. The idea is to re-create the basic subdermal support for the skin, if it has been damaged by accident. The two layers of the skin are the epidermis on the surface and the dermis below (see diagram on page 60). The dermis gives the skin its substance and support. To re-create this support, we take a "deep dermal stitch," a suture deep inside the wound, through the dermis, to prevent the wound from widening. This reduces the pulling-apart tension on the skin so that the process of growing new skin can begin.

The three-layer approach is often the best for treating soft tissue injuries. The deep dermal stitch keeps the wound from widening.

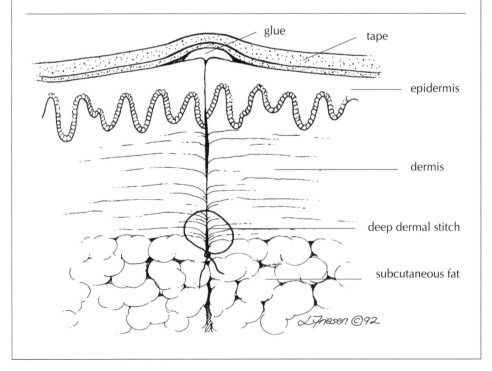

Great advances have been made in the kind of sutures we are able to apply to the deep dermal stitch. We now have suture materials that allow the stitch to retain its tensile strength for a good sixty days, then slowly mix with the water in the body to dissolve out, or disappear within about 180 days.

The needle used for a deep dermal stitch is shaped like part of a circle. These needles come in quarter circle, three-eighths circle and half-circle sizes. Their shape makes it easier to work in tiny spaces, but the ultimate skill lies with the surgeon: there should be as few sutures as possible, and they should not be drawn too tightly or the blood flow will be restricted and this will slow the healing process.

In most cases, we take a three-layer approach to closing up a wound. After the deep dermal stitch, the surface or second layer stitch is taken. This is a suture that makes the skin edges level with one another. It's a loose stitch designed to make the meeting of the edges

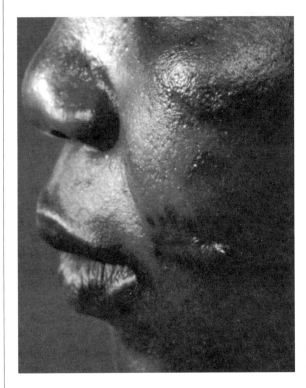

If surface stitches stay in too long, the skin may create a scarring pattern called railway tracking.

as flat as possible, rather than to hold the edges together. For this suture, we use a fast-absorbing gut that will dissolve out in five days, as long as it is covered. Unfortunately, some patients may end up in emergency rooms equipped with non-absorbing sutures and, unless they get these surface stitches removed within five days, they can suffer cross-hatch scars.

Cross-hatching comes about when the stitches stay in too long and the new skin begins to migrate *down* the sutures. This creates tiny holes. If there are other sutures laid across the wound, they'll create scarring in another pattern that we call "railway tracking." Over the years, I've had to help several patients with scarring created by sutures left in too long. Some surgeons avoid the whole problem of sutures by using Histoacryl glue to set the edges of the wound evenly. I personally prefer the use of the deep dermal stitch to keep the wound edges as narrow as possible.

The "third layer" to close up a wound is actually anti-tension tape applied to the surface of the skin. The tape is used to compress the wound so that, again, its tendency to widen is curtailed. Depending on the type of wound and its severity, this taping might be applied for as long as two months after the operation to maintain a narrow edge.

In an abrasion type of skin injury, a scrape, there might be a lot of foreign particles imbedded in the dermal layer of skin — too many to be removed by the cleansing wash of peroxide. In this case, we might have to do a bit of dermabrading to remove all the foreign particles. Otherwise, the particles will result in a tattoo type of scarring when the wound heals.

Wounding to the ears, nostrils or lips demands special cosmetic consideration. If an ear has been partly torn away, for example, the chief concern is to sew the lobe and cartilage parts back into their natural position. If the outside edge of the ear, the helical rim, is not properly restored anatomically, a large "notching" deformity will become noticeable. Likewise, we try to match up the nostrils and avoid notching at the base of each nostril by lining up the rims in their natural positions.

The lips are a challenge because it's important that the vermilion border (junction of dark and fleshtone lip) is restored to its original place. We also want to avoid the situation where a lip scar becomes very noticeable if a patient "animates" by smiling, or puckering up. This can happen if the muscle underneath the skin hasn't been properly sewn. The area surrounding the lips is one of the few places on the body where the skin is directly attached to the muscle, so we really can't fix one without the other.

If, despite our best efforts, a facial wound becomes infected, symptoms such as inflammation, reddening and painful swelling will appear within seventy-two hours. If the infection is caught early, and it isn't too deep, it usually can be brought under control with penicillin or other oral antibiotics. But if an abscess forms deep in the wound, then the wound must be opened up and drained. Either way, infection is something that every emergency officer, or doctor, tries to avoid because the resulting inflammation will contribute to more scarring.

Another possible outcome of facial scarring is the development of "hypertrophic" scars and "keloids." Hypertrophic means thickened; these scars represent an abnormally thick and tough response to wounding. Keloids come about when the scar tissue begins to expand beyond the borders of the original wound. I've seen the tiny scar in a pierced earlobe grow to the size of a robin's egg. Statistically, hypertrophic scarring and keloids are more likely to plague certain races: people of Asian, Negroid or South Mediterranean Caucasian extraction.

If keloids or hypertrophic scars begin to appear during the healing process, there are a few things we can do. The best method of treatment is to make injections of triamcinolone acetonide, known as Kenalog. Kenalog is the steroid noted earlier that works to dissolve scars. We can start the injections at the time of closing the wound or early in the healing process if keloids start to form. The injections are repeated at least once a month until the scar stops thickening. Hypertrophic scars respond a little more quickly to the injections than keloids, but it is important not to overdo the treatment. Too much Kenalog can result in a loss of pigment or "dermal atrophy," meaning the skin in the area will be thinned and begin to look depressed.

Another method of treatment is to try cutting out the hypertrophic scars or keloids. Unfortunately, this isn't always effective because, of course, the same racial factors apply to the new scar created by the excision. In fact, some doctors have reported that up to fifty-five percent of their patients simply redevelop the problem. However, the resultant scar after surgery is usually cosmetically more appealing to the eye.

Lastly, we can apply special pressure dressings that will, ultimately, make the scars more aesthetically acceptable. The catch is that such dressings must exert true pressure to be effective and they must be applied day and night for a minimum of six months to one year. The dressings cannot be removed for any period of time longer than thirty minutes. Obviously, this is a very restrictive form of treatment and impractical for use in the head and neck area.

Scar Repair

So far, I've talked about the immediate reaction to wounding of facial soft tissue. As you can see, our motivation is to minimize the scarring that will form as the body heals. But, as I said, skilled cosmetic surgeons are not always on the front line in the emergency room. Scar camouflage surgery is **not** performed at the time of initial repair. For most facial lacerations, the emergency doctor is well trained to sew up the patient and recommend follow-up visits to a cosmetic surgeon for possible scar revision. Scar revision, or linear scar revision as it is called, is one of the major areas of study in our field.

Before we can work to camouflage unacceptable scarring on the face, the original scars must mature. This involves the "six and six" rule that I have mentioned previously: at six weeks, a scar will look its worst (very red); at six months, the scar starts to mature. A mature scar is white and sometimes barely noticeable. Obviously, it is in everyone's best interest to wait and see how the original scarring matures. It might fade to the point that no cosmetic revision is necessary.

We have a set of general guidelines as to what makes a "good" scar, whether it be formed by accident or through surgery. A good scar must be level with its surrounding skin; it should not be higher than adjacent areas, nor in a depression deeper than half a millime-

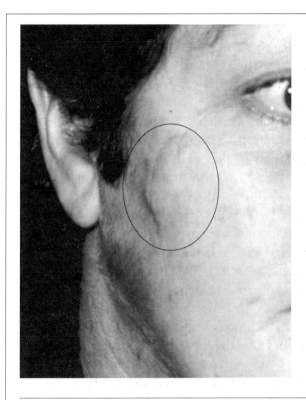

C shaped wounds can become a problem when the surface inside the circle becomes raised during healing.

ter. A good scar is no wider than two millimeters, but its length can vary depending on where it appears on the face.

If the scar is at the junction of two regional aesthetic units, say the cheek and the nose, and it happens to lie exactly within the junction line, a good scar can be very long and still be inconspicuous. When a scar forms within a single aesthetic unit, length can be more of a problem. Within the region of the forehead, a good scar could be long and barely noticeable: if it were horizontal, tucked into one of the relaxed skin tension lines and level with the surrounding skin, the length really wouldn't matter. But in the region of the cheek, a good scar can't be longer than one-and-a-half centimeters, or it is too easily identifiable to the eye.

A good scar should heal without contracting, or else it will "pull" at the borders of regional aesthetic units, as I mentioned above. Mature scars are without pigment, which makes them easy to see in darker-skinned people if the scars are too wide or too long. A good scar should allow normal facial movement, which again might be a problem if the scar transverses two regional aesthetic units, or if a laceration to the lip has been improperly repaired.

There are many types of problem scars, or "bad" scars, including scars that lack the desirable characteristics I've talked about. Other problem scars include the traumatic scar shaped like a C or a half-circle — often on the forehead — that heals by raising the surface inside the circle. This is what we call the "trapdoor" phenomenon. Scarring in the inner canthal area, the inside corner of the eye where the upper and lower lids meet, sometimes results in a "web" scar that creates an Oriental type of appearance with an epicanthal fold. And a scar that transverses the mandibular line of the lower jaw often will form a deep depression.

Our purpose, when we approach a patient with matured problem scarring, is to revise the scars, or transform them into "good" scars. Keep in mind, the cosmetic surgeon's skill is to be able to deceive the eye; the scars are not removed, they are camouflaged.

There are four basic techniques that can be used to camouflage scars: simple excision; excision and moving the scar to the relaxed skin tension lines; breaking up the scar; and skin leveling, or dermabrasion.

Excision

Simple excision is used mostly on scars that are too wide. We cut out the existing scar and then sew up the resulting wound, using the three-level approach that I described above of a deep dermal stitch, superficial stitch and taping. The original wound might have resulted in a wide scar because the skin was ruptured or lacerated by a blow or a jagged instrument in an accident. When we excise the scar and re-create the wound, the conditions are much more controlled as we use a scalpel to do the cutting. The cleaner edges of the wound will heal in a more level fashion.

Years ago, the technique of "serial excisions" was popular for large areas of scarring. This kind of scarring might result from a bad bout with skin cancer, for example. The idea was to cut out the scarring, apply a large skin graft, then every six months or so, in a series of

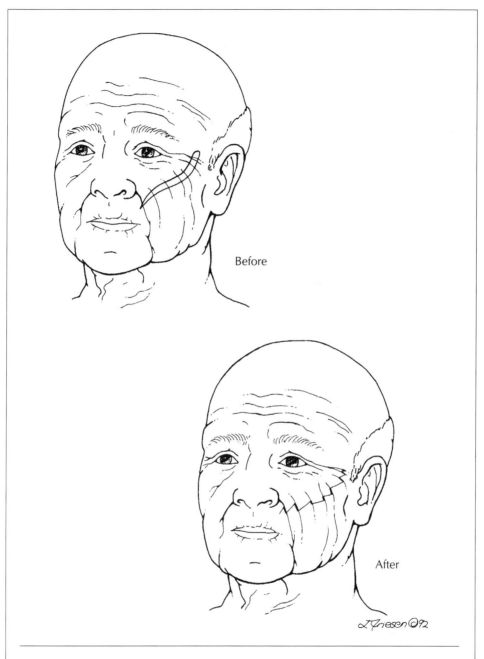

Before

After

When a large scar crosses more than one aesthetic unit and several facial dynamic lines, we can make it less noticeable by breaking the scar up with a series of smaller scars and deceiving the eye.

operations, cut out a bit of the graft and sew up the resulting wound. The intervals between operations allowed new skin to stretch and grow into place. This way, the edges of the normal surrounding skin were gradually brought together and the graft was eventually made inconspicuous.

Today, faced with a large area of scarring, we use "tissue expanders" instead. These are silicone bags gradually filled with normal saline (saltwater) that are inserted under the skin. They stay in place just long enough for the dermis to regenerate and stretch over the bags so that there is enough local new skin to cover the defect or widened scar. It's an unsightly process — patients can be grossly malformed by the very large bags — but well worth the temporary discomfort of six weeks or so. When we remove the bags, there is an entire new flap of the patient's own skin that we can use to cover the area that was scarred.

The second technique to camouflage a scar is to excise the old scar and then move a new, surgically created scar closer to the nearest relaxed skin tension line. Let's say, for example, that a patient had suffered a cancerous tumor on the nose that had had to be removed and patched up with skin grafts, creating a very noticeable scar. What I might do in this instance is cut out the graft scarring in the middle of the nose, then rotate adjacent skin to cover the exposed area. This would create thin linear scars where they are more easily camouflaged at the junction of nearby regional aesthetic units, like the nose-cheek grooves.

Scar Transformation

Breaking up the scar, our third camouflage technique, involves using a combination of geometric cuts that we refer to as Z-plasties, W-plasties and M-plasties. The letters Z, W and M resemble the shape of the cuts; plasties is a plural word derived from the Latin and Greek words for plastic, as in plastic surgery. (There are other, less commonly used cuts also referred to by their shapes, such as the "V to Y advancement" technique. The names are simply shorthand to quickly describe the kind of cut we are going to make.) Once the skin has been geometrically cut, we swivel it around to change the direction of an existing scar.

As an example, if a patient had a five-centimeter horizontal scar across the cheek, we could make it less noticeable by breaking it up with a "running W-plasty" cut. This is a series of W-plasties, slightly angled, that transform the scar from a single line into small segments of scarring. Some of the W-plasties could be made parallel with existing facial lines, further camouflaging the scar. We might mix in a couple of M and Z-plasties to break up the scar even more. The end result would be a rough patch of skin with tiny asymmetrical scars, instead of an unbroken gash. Many factors affect the quality of the end result, including the type of skin a patient had to begin with, but I've seen this technique work wonders on some thin to medium thick-skinned people.

The large scar is excised and broken up with a series of M and W-plasties (geometric cuts) that help the scar to lie flat.

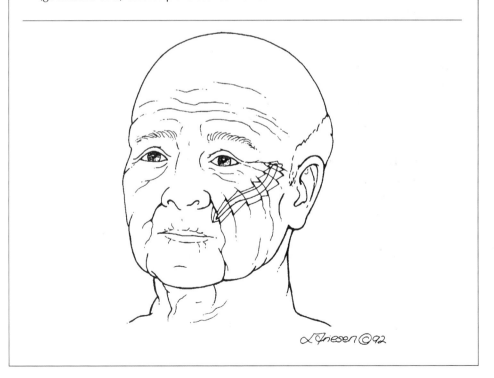

Breaking up a scar is also an effective way to treat some of the special situations I mentioned above — problem scars like the "trapdoor" phenomenon or webbing in the corner of the eye. A web is created when a scar contracts during healing. The challenge is to ease the pulling caused by contraction and flatten the scar. A Z-plasty cut solves the problem by allowing the skin to be rearranged in a geometric fashion. We are able to increase the distance between two points by cutting in a Z-shape, and this allows the scar to lie flat.

The "trapdoor" phenomenon requires a combination of techniques. This is because a trapdoor involves two types of scarring: the linear scar that outlines the edges, and the scarring underneath that is contracting and causing the area to bulge out from the surrounding skin. We start by cutting Z-plasties into the corners of the scar, then pulling up the skin to "undermine" beneath the scar and on the outside of the trapdoor. The trapdoor area collapses and the Z-plasties allow us to sew the skin flat.

Dermabrasion

Dermabrasion is used for accidental scarring much as I described in detail in the chapter on scarring caused by acne. If a scar is a little depressed, we can dermabrade the surrounding skin to make it level. Or we can dermabrade the scar itself if it is higher than the surrounding skin — shave it down a bit. Dermabrasion is often best combined with some collagen injections, to completely smooth out the affected area. This might, for example, be the solution for a scar that is in a relaxed skin tension line in the forehead or cheek regional aesthetic units. Almost all facial scars can be made smoother and more level with dermabrasion.

There have been such advances in our ability to camouflage scarring that it gives me pleasure to say one of my most satisfied patients is a woman who survived a near-fatal car accident. She came to me with ghastly scars on her forehead, caused by wounding when she went through the windshield. It took two years to complete a series of scar repositions before we got the jagged, uneven gashes moved into the horizontal lines of her natural forehead wrinkles. The scars that couldn't be moved were dermabraded for a smooth finish. Today, this particular patient's scars are barely noticeable. Cases like hers are what keep facial cosmetic surgeons wedded to their work; we all love a happy ending.

CHAPTER SIX

The Face-lift

O F ALL THE THINGS that a cosmetic facial surgeon can do for people, the face-lift is surely the most talked-about. Perhaps it's because some entertainers have so long been associated with this particular operation. Singers and dancers and actors, by virtue of the business they are in, often are insecure about aging and obsessed with their appearance. Maybe it's this connection that makes the face-lift so controversial. But not everyone who decides to get a face-lift is driven by such extreme forces.

In a certain sense, a face-lift is one of the more innocuous procedures that a patient can choose. People who turn to plastic surgery for a hair transplant, or perhaps a new nose, are looking for a dramatic improvement in their appearance: a change. This is different from what most people want from a face-lift. When these people look in the mirror, their aging appearance does not match up with their psychological impression of themselves. This impression is sometimes referred to as the "body image." They want the image in the mirror to reflect their psychological self-portrait.

Sometimes people seek out a face-lift as a reaction to the death of or separation from a spouse; it's an attempt to put things back the way they were before a tragedy. These patients need grief counseling before they consider a face-lift. As I explained in the introductory chapter, cosmetic surgeons devote a lot of time to screening potential

The pre-operative (left) and post-operative views of a total facial rejuvenation, including face-lift, liposuction, and implants in lip cheek grooves and the mid-cheek region.

candidates for surgery, and this is one area in which we are particularly cautious. A mid-life crisis must be separated from simple dissatisfaction with a middle-aged appearance.

The earlier a patient has a face-lift, the more frequently the procedure will have to be repeated to maintain the desired effect. A "middle-aged" patient of forty-three may want to restore a look with hardly any sag at all, to recapture a thirtyish appearance. This would mean the procedure would have to be repeated five years later. But if patients wait until they are about fifty-five, when they have come to accept a bit of natural sag and wrinkling, it will likely be a one-time operation. A rough estimate is that if you get a face-lift at forty, it will last five years; at fifty, it will last seven to ten years; at fifty-five, it will last a lifetime. Cosmetic surgeons have a jaunty little expression that sums it up: "Recurrence begins as the last stitch goes in."

As I mentioned earlier, everyone ages at an individual rate, but there are some generally applicable periods when aging is gradual or accelerated. Most people age gradually to about age fifty. The aging process accelerates between fifty and sixty, then "plateaus" between sixty and seventy. After seventy, the process speeds up again. A patient's rate of aging might have a bearing on the best time to have a face-lift.

Studies have been published that examine the connection between a patient's psychological health and the desire for a face-lift. In 1935, *The Journal of Applied Psychology* published a piece by psychologist C. Buhler as to what constitutes a healthy, well-adjusted, middle-aged person; this piece has become something of a benchmark against which to measure the motivations of candidates for a face-lift.

According to Buhler, valuable assets in coping with middle age include a flexible attitude toward others, a variety of interests, a healthy self-regard, a willingness to accept help from others and a realistic assessment of one's own abilities. In my experience, most face-lift patients may be slightly deficient in one or more of these areas.

The results of many cosmetic surgery operations help to build self-esteem, though few are as effective as the face-lift. Four out of five face-lift patients treated in my office are women, but I'll use the example of a widower to illustrate my point. When he first came to see me, this middle-aged gentleman had lost his wife a year earlier. He was having a lot of trouble reaching out to make friends and socialize. We agreed on a face-lift, and he has since begun to date and enjoy life again. The truth is, the face-lift changed his self-esteem more than it changed his appearance. His confidence got a big boost.

Lower Face-lift

In the early 1960s, surgeons thought of the face-lift operation as being so long and difficult that it was necessary to do one side of the face one day, then the other side a day later. Dr. Jack Anderson, one of my mentors during my fellowship, told me this years ago. I have never experienced this approach, though I have since seen a slide presentation of a patient whose father died in the middle of her surgery and she had to almost literally get up from the operating room table to attend to the funeral arrangements. For eight months, she went about with half her face-lifted. It became an interesting sort of controlled study of the face-lift techniques back then, because the half lift held up quite well for that eight months.

Prior to the early 1970s, a face-lift was not nearly as effective, or lasting, as it is today, even though it involved more surgery. We had an expression for the extent of the cutting that we had to do: the surgeon and his assistant would "shake hands" underneath the skin beneath the chin by the time dissection was complete. We'd cut all the way down the side of the face, underneath the chin, loosen the skin completely and pull it up. This was known as the full face-lift operation; a simple tightening of the skin over the cheek and upper neck. Although the results were aesthetically pleasing, the extent of surgery performed with this method led to a much higher rate of postoperative complications.

A double layer face-lift lifts both the SMAS fascia (the underlying connective tissue) and the outer skin.

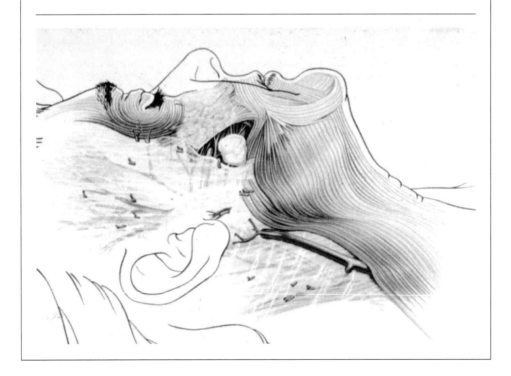

Some surgeons had experimented with techniques that gave support to the underlying structures of the face in the 1960s and 1970s, but the attempts were random and not always effective. The profession had begun to realize that just pulling back the skin wasn't enough to secure a face-lift. In 1976, an article titled "The Superficial Musculo-Aponeurotic System (SMAS) in the Parotid and Cheek Area," by Dr. V. Mitz and Dr. M. Peyronie, appeared in *The Plastic Reconstructive Surgery Journal*, and the face-lift operation was forever changed. The article confirmed that underlying sinew and muscles also needed surgery to make a face-lift last.

In the previous chapter on aging skin, I mentioned that the SMAS fascia, as it is often referred to, is a delicate sheath of connective tissue that lies between the deepest layer of skin (the dermis) and the underlying glands and muscles. In a paper I prepared with Dr. Larry J. Shemen for *The Journal of Otolaryngology* in 1981, titled "Use of the Fascial Plane System in the Face-lift Operation," we explained that definitions of the SMAS fascia vary. Some researchers in the field refer to it as loose, connective tissue; others see it as dense, irregularly arranged connective tissue. However it is defined, SMAS fascia is made of large, thick collagen fibers, mixed with thin, wavy elastic fibers, fatty tissue and fibroblasts. Fibroblasts are cells that create connective tissue fibers.

As it ages, the SMAS fascia loses its elasticity and begins to sag. Until this phenomenon was properly understood, surgeons were treating only the skin for its sag without addressing the SMAS fascia. As a result, no matter how tightly the skin was pulled, the SMAS fascia would counteract the face-lift and begin to reveal sag again within a couple of years. (In fairness to those who had the procedure done in the 1960s, this might be where they got the idea that they had to have repeated face-lifts to maintain their appearance.)

The SMAS fascia is directly attached to the platysma, which is the broad, thin muscle on either side of the neck. It extends from the top part of each shoulder all the way up over either side of the jawline. When the platysma is in an advanced state of sagging, toward the middle of the fifties in most people, but, surprisingly, occurring much earlier in others, you'll see two "cords" begin to

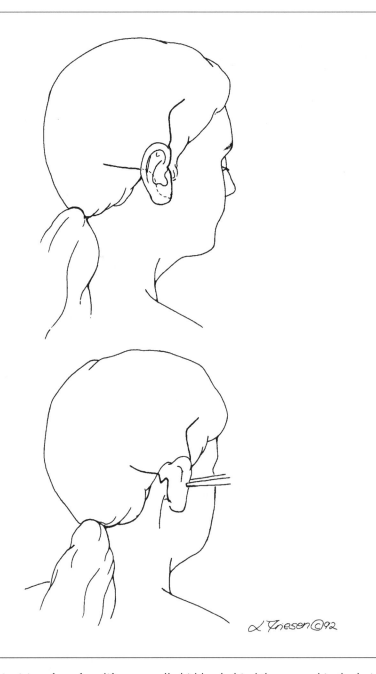

The incisions for a face-lift are usually hidden behind the ear and in the hair-line. The incisions are different for male and female patients.

appear at the front of the neck. These cords are actually the leading front edges of the platysma muscle, which has fallen forward with the fascia. A face-lift operation takes into account both the cheek and neck areas, so that, again, the SMAS fascia and its effect on the platysma is an important factor.

Because of our advanced understanding of the SMAS fascia, we almost always perform what is known as the "two-layer" face-lift when the operation is called for. There are several ways of dealing with the two layers of skin and SMAS fascia, and new techniques are continually being introduced as we get to better understand these remarkable body organs. For example, different procedures are employed for patients who smoke: their micro-circulation is reduced as a result of smoking, and the skin will not tolerate much pull.

Generally speaking, the most common approach is to loosen and lift both the skin and the SMAS fascia underneath before snipping off the excess in both layers and suturing up afterward. In my experience, this is a safe and effective technique, and the face-lift lasts a good long time. The interesting thing is that the two-layer approach requires less surgery for better results. No more "shaking hands" under the chin skin!

The incisions we make for a face-lift vary slightly from surgeon to surgeon. Many surgeons actually draw lines with felt-tip pen indicating where we plan to cut on the patient's face. This is done when the patient is sitting upright on the operating table so that we can trace the areas of sag. (As soon as the patient lies down, these areas disappear or fall away to the sides of the face.) Some surgeons simply prefer one type of cut over another, so the lines are not always exactly the same. And the lines will vary depending on what the patient has to offer in terms of hairline, fatty deposits and other factors.

The incision starts with a continuous cut around the ear that starts in front of and above the ear (in the hairline), traveling down in front of the ear underneath the lobe, then up behind the ear, tracing the ridge of cartilage to the mastoid bone, just above and back of the ear. At a point level with the top of the ear canal, the incision travels straight back horizontally into the hair.

When this cut has been completed, I loosen the skin and the SMAS fascia separately, then pull them up. By pulling up, the extra tissue that sags becomes apparent when it overlaps the cut lines. This is the tissue that we excise, or snip off. The resulting wound is then sutured, using the method I described earlier in the chapter on linear scar revision. (This is a three-layer approach to closing a wound, with a deep dermal stitch, surface stitching or Histoacryl glue, then temporary taping to hold everything in place.)

The incision behind the ear allows access so that a surgeon can correct sag in the neck and lower chin area. If the patient has trouble with "cording" in the neck — meaning the SMAS fascia has sagged and brought forward the leading edges of the platysmal muscles as I explained above — I will use this incision to reach down and pull up the muscles, anchoring them with sutures as close to the mastoid as possible.

The incision in front of the ear deals with sag that is above the chin, but still within the lower half of the face. This is the kind of sag that often reveals itself in a deep lip-cheek groove where the cheek mound has sagged forward and down. The cut continues at the bottom of the ear, behind the lobe, where the posterior cut ended. The scalpel traces a line that travels up the front of the ear, as close as possible to the base of the tragus (the cartilage shutter at the front of the ear that you can push in to block out loud sounds), then disappears vertically into the hairline.

If you look carefully, you'll see a slight natural angle between the cheek and the tragus, and by cutting along the base, the resulting scar, when it heals, will contract to maintain this angle. Occasionally, I will make an incision behind the tragus, then add a deep suture to give the area a natural-looking cheek-tragal angle after surgery.

When both the skin and the SMAS fascia are pulled up toward the hairline, the extra tissue is revealed at the cut by the way it overlaps the ear. The extra tissue is excised and the wound sutured, as I described above. This procedure can result in the lip-cheek groove being diminished by up to fifty percent; a dramatic result. Any remaining groove can be filled in with collagen or Gore-Tex.

Some surgeons extend the incision above the area of the temples in the hairline. They'll pull up from this area to correct sag in the upper

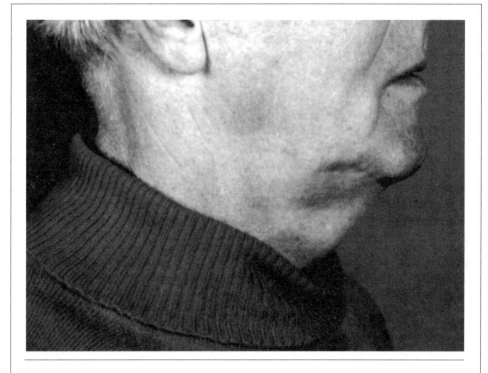

The jowly look occurs when fat deposits along the jawline and under the chin magnify the sag of skin and the SMAS fascia; liposuction and a face-lift can be used to treat the problem.

third of the face, especially around the eyes and the lateral eyebrow area. I rarely perform this temporal lift only because I find sagging in this area is more effectively treated with a forehead-lift. The face-lift and the forehead-lift are two different operations, and each one creates a different effect; often, I'll perform both as a combined procedure. (For more information on the forehead-lift, see Chapter Three: The Eye Region.)

Liposuction

Another complementary procedure to the face-lift operation is liposuction along the jaw-line. This is because patients who need a face-lift often show a tendency toward being "jowly." Jowls are created when the SMAS fascia and the skin sag, and the problem is made worse with local deposits of fat along the jaw-line. It's a kind of hangdog look, and both men and women suffer from it. (Younger patients can often be treated with a liposuction alone; they don't yet have the problems of sagging to correct.)

For those who need it, liposuction and a face-lift can be done as a continuous procedure. I start by making three incisions for the lipo-suction. No incision is more than about one-and-a-half centimeters long, which minimizes scarring afterward. The first incision is made one centimeter under the chin. The next two are made behind each earlobe. (You might have noticed that the ears are terrific hiding places for most of the scarring associated with face-lifts.) Operating from three incisions facilitates the removal of fat from the jowls and prevents taking too much fat from under the chin area; it gives a more balanced contour to the neck and jaw.

Through these incisions, I insert a hollow metal tube called a cannula, which is connected to plastic tubing and a motor-driven vacuum. In a kind of fanlike motion, I work the cannula just under the skin to suck out the fatty deposits. People are always surprised at how vigorous an action this is, but the short, sharp, smooth strokes are needed to break up tissue, and it's a smoother technique than it appears to be. During the procedure, patients are awake but sedated in most cases; some prefer a general anesthetic. Either way, patients feel no pain, though they might react to the curious, sucking sound that the vacuum makes. The cannula is designed to extract only fat, which travels in globules down the tubing to a receptacle. Once I've got all the fat out, we can see the true extent of sagging to be repaired by face-lift. (If the patient is younger, the skin will contract or shrink on its own, making a face-lift unnecessary.)

Maintaining the natural hairline behind the ear is an important element of any face-lift operation, whether the patient is male or female. Years ago, we used to bring the incision behind the ear down along the hairline, and the resultant scar became visible with a short haircut, or with long hair pulled back into a ponytail. Now, as I described above, we take the incision straight back into the hair, and this has pretty well eliminated the problem.

Men can be a bit of a challenge in a face-lift operation because of some of their hair-growth patterns. A surgeon has to be careful not to draw back the sideburn hair so far that it looks unnaturally thinned. The skin behind men's ears is non-hair-bearing, but when the skin is pulled back and upward during a face-lift, the hair-bearing skin just below the ear moves behind the earlobe. This area must be shaved.

The progress we've made by treating both the SMAS fascia and the skin with a face-lift has lessened the likelihood of postoperative complications. There is less surface area of surgery and therefore less chance of bleeding or "hematoma formation" when pools of blood collect under the skin. There have been rare cases, however, where a surgeon has damaged one of the branches of facial nerves that provide movement to the face.

Facial cosmetic surgeons will continue to offer the "two-layer" face-lift with liposuction because of the enormous improvement over the previous method when only the skin was treated. This approach results in a longer-lasting lift, and our ability to reduce the depth of the lip-cheek groove is much improved. The SMAS fascia can be tightened in a different direction than the skin layer, which enhances the effect of the lift and makes the skin more flexible. But it also seems to result in less swelling over a shorter period of time — in fact, the entire healing process is faster and better after this operation — again, because there is less surgery involved.

During recovery from a face-lift operation, patients are likely to experience some "hypoesthesia." This is a temporary loss of sensation, or a numb feeling, and there are a couple of reasons for it. The natural swelling following the operation might contribute to hypoesthesia — much the same way your face feels numb for a while after someone has slapped it. If the feeling of numbness is localized around the lower part of the ear and the earlobe, it could be that the nerves to these parts of the ear were separated in order to do the lift. Either way, hypoesthesia often disappears after six weeks and rarely lasts as long as six months.

Patients recovering from a face-lift must wear a firmly wrapped tensor bandage continuously — night and day — for two weeks following surgery. The extensive wrapping resembles a football helmet with a chin "sling." The purpose of the bandage is to counter the effects of the swelling that naturally occurs after surgery; without it, the swelling may stretch the skin and cause renewed sagging.

The Chin

I'll end this chapter by mentioning a couple of uncommon circumstances related to the face-lift procedure. For example, there is the rare patient who has unusually saggy skin — the classic "turkey" neck, or wattle under the chin — and all the pulling up in the world won't correct the sag under the chin. The basic principle is, the further away you are from the pull, the less the effect. In this case, we might be forced to make an incision under the chin and excise some skin from there, too.

Another circumstance comes about when a patient approaches me for a face-lift, and it is clear there are other problems I could deal with at the same time. A good example is the patient who has a receding chin combined with sagging jowls, which often makes the person look rather "owlish." I will take the time to explain that once we've made the incisions for the face-lift, we might just as well put an implant under the skin in front of the chin and jowl area before sewing up. These implants are made of flexible, solid, medical-grade plastic, and they come in a variety of shapes that fit over the existing chin bone. (Shapes that resemble the rinds of orange, grapefruit or lemon slices.) A face-lift might also give us the opportunity to do cheek implants, creating more pronounced, "higher" cheekbones or correcting a mid-face collapse.

As I mentioned, most face-lift patients are looking to capture the psychological image that they have of themselves, and a stronger chin or more noticeable cheekbones might not fit that image. But if a patient is afflicted with mid-cheek hollowing for example, an implant might be the icing on the cake to achieve the more youthful appearance of a fuller cheek and lifted face. As a facial cosmetic surgeon, I consider it part of my commitment to educate patients about the procedures and alternatives that will produce the most pleasing effect.

CHAPTER SEVEN

The Lips

YOU MIGHT SAY that lips form the uppermost end of the aerodigestive tract, and you'd be right, but poetry has been written about the way these parts of the tract affect our lives, and loves. Lips are the visual expression of our emotions. You know when someone is angry by the way their lips are drawn into a thin line; you know when someone is amorous by the way they plump and pucker. Lips are important to speech, especially pronunciation. And they are sensitive erogenous zones, which is why kissing is so popular.

There are several reasons why people seek out the services of a cosmetic facial surgeon when it comes to their lips. Some have suffered an injury and ended up with scarring on the lips — like the arrow through Cupid's heart. Others have developed paralysis, and with it, a shyness, because their lips pull into alarming contortions when they smile. Some want the cosmetic boost of a collagen injection for lips like Barbara Hershey's in the movie "Beaches." Hershey lips; Hershey kisses. Before I explain how a cosmetic surgeon can help, it might be a good idea to describe exactly what lips are.

The Shape

Lips are upper and lower parts divided by the "oral orifice": the mouth. Each part is further divided into red and white segments at what is called the "vermilion border." This border is well defined by the contrast in colors and by the change in skin texture. The color contrast is most noticeable in Caucasians: the white flesh part of the lip blends with the skin of the face; the red part is a thin membrane, rich with blood. When you look at someone from the side, the red segments are more noticeable than the flesh because they project further from the face in a kind of pout. Cosmetic surgeons describe the lips as arching backward. The lips are joined together at the "commissures," otherwise known as the corners of your mouth.

The skin of the upper lip hangs like a curtain from the base of the nose. It is defined on either side by the lip-cheek grooves. In the middle of the flesh-colored upper lip, there is a vertical depression

Anatomy of the lips

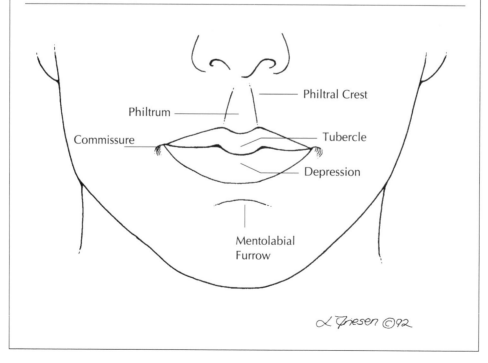

called the "philtrum," which is accentuated on each side by "philtral crests"; the philtral area resembles one of the decorative depressions you make in the edges of a piecrust.

The red upper lip has two lateral wings with a small red nodule in the middle, called a "tubercle," that hangs over a corresponding groove in the lower lip. The place where the red and flesh-colored skins of the upper lip join is shaped like a flattened M and it is called the "Cupid's bow." Few other places on the body are as important to our sense of sexuality as this seven millimeters of skin.

The flesh-colored segment of the lower lip is anchored to the chin by a horseshoe-shaped groove just under the middle of the red segment. Again, the lip is defined on either side by the chin-cheek grooves. The red segment of the lower lip has two lateral lobes (fuller than the lateral wings of the upper lip), joined by a shallow groove in the middle. When the upper and lower lips are at rest, they should just touch each other, without a gap.

This kind of technical description should offer a new perspective on the popular romance-novel expression, "she parted her lips." She parts them, puckers them, smiles, or does anything else with her lips by using ten muscles paired into five groups: those that raise the upper lip; those that raise the commissures, or corners; those that pull down the commissures; those that pull down the lower lip; and those that act to contract the circumference of the lips as a unit.

Depending on how these groups of muscles are used, they will interact to produce the three classic smiles that a human being is capable of: the Mona Lisa smile; the canine smile; and the full dental smile. The Mona Lisa smile is characterised by a minimal display of teeth. It is similar to the enigmatic smile in the famous Mona Lisa portrait by Leonardo da Vinci. Interestingly, this small smile requires the use of the three paired muscles coming from the cheekbone. Perhaps this is why such a smile is sometimes referred to as "strained." The canine smile is known as a more aggressive smile; it shows more of the upper front teeth. And the full dental smile, as its name implies, shows both the upper and lower teeth — it is generally the last smiling step on the way to an all-out, open-mouthed laugh.

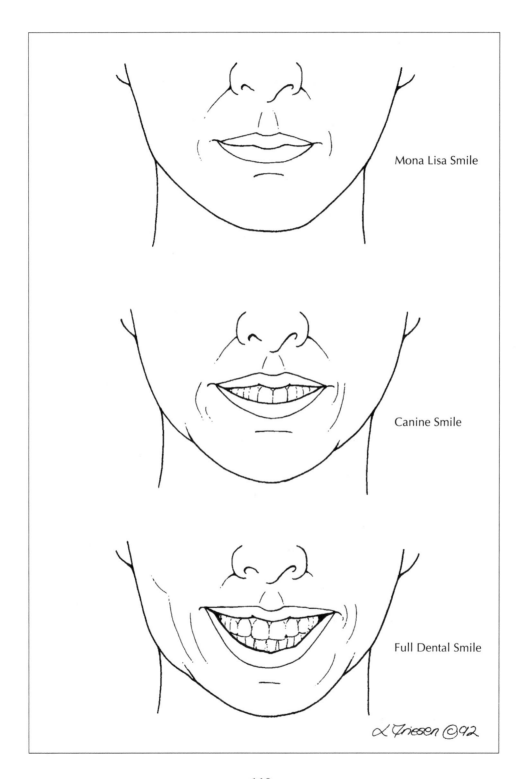

Mona Lisa Smile

Canine Smile

Full Dental Smile

L Friesen ©92

As I mentioned in an earlier chapter on facial assessment, a well-proportioned face should divide into three equal parts, measured from the hairline to the top of the eyebrows, from the eyebrows to the bottom of the nose, and from there to the bottom of the chin. Lips, which occupy the bottom one-third of the face, should be measured for proportion starting at the exact point where the "tubercle" (the small nodule of flesh that sits at the center of the upper lip) meets the corresponding shallow groove in the lower lip. Up from this point to the bottom of the nose should measure one-third of the bottom third of the overall face; down from this point to the bottom of the chin should measure two-thirds of the bottom third.

There are other ways to measure proportion in the area of the lips, many of them named for their inventors. For example, the Frankfort plane, which is a straight, horizontal line drawn from the front of the ear, will intersect with the Gonzalez-Uloa zero meridi-

Lips, which occupy the bottom one-third of the face, should also be measured for proportion.

an line to reveal whether or not the chin is too prominent in the bottom third of the face. (See below.) Legan's angle of facial convexity, on the other hand, measures the projection of soft tissues, like lips, in the bottom third, while Rickett's E-line measures the relationship of the upper lip to the lower lip. By adulthood, the upper lip should be about four millimeters behind the E-line; the lower lip should be about two millimeters behind.

What Can Be Done

Most cosmetic surgeons will try to view the lips in the context of the entire lower third of the face, and this involves an assessment of the neck and chin. The chin is second only to the nose in its importance to the human face. A "strong" or prominent chin is seen as a sign of

When assessing the chin in proportion with the lower third of the face, we often use the intersection of the Frankfort plane and the Gonzalez-Uloa zero meridian line as a guide.

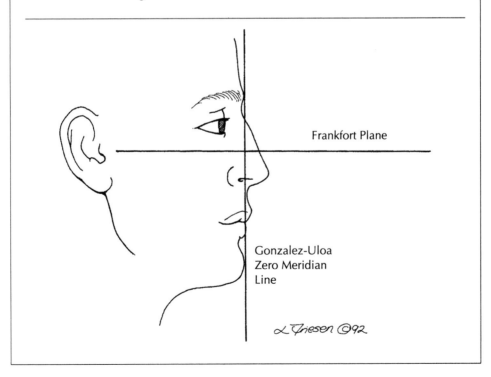

Frankfort Plane

Gonzalez-Uloa
Zero Meridian
Line

strong character. Likewise, a "weak" or receding chin leaves the impression that a person is a ditherer, of low resolve. (Look no further than two contemporary Canadian politicians for an illustration of public perception on the matter: both prime minister Brian Mulroney and former prime minister Joe Clark have "taken it on the chin" for their prominent and not-so-prominent chins.)

The chin profile is largely determined by the angle at which it meets the neck. The neck-chin junction, as it is called, is the angle created by the underside of the chin (where you hold a buttercup to see if someone likes butter, according to an old adage) and the front of the neck, down to the Adam's apple. There is a system of categorizing the relationship of the neck to the chin, called the Dedo classification. These six classes are based on the degree of looseness in the skin, fat accumulation, bone position and "retrognathia" — the orthodontic situation when the upper jaw is normal in size and the lower jaw is so much smaller and farther back that it prevents the teeth from fitting together properly.

Dedo also takes into account the tone of the platysma muscle, which I described in the chapters on aging skin and the face-lift. With age, the platysma muscle sags forward on either side of the neck and it creates what looks like "cords"; this can be corrected with a face-lift.

Class 1, according to Dedo, defines a patient with good platysma muscle tone, little neck fat and a normal neck-chin angle; this patient would be an unlikely candidate for cosmetic surgery. Class 2 is a patient with some sagging skin in the neck-chin area, but no extra fat or platysma "cording"; a face-lift would probably correct the problem. Class 3 is a patient with excessive fat under the chin, which obliterates the normal neck-chin angle. This requires a submental liposuction (liposuction under the chin) and a face-lift because the patient's skin would not contract. Class 4 is a patient who shows the classic platysmal "cording"; as I mentioned, this problem can be corrected during the face-lift operation. Classes 5 and 6 are patients with structural problems deeper than the soft tissue of the neck and chin.

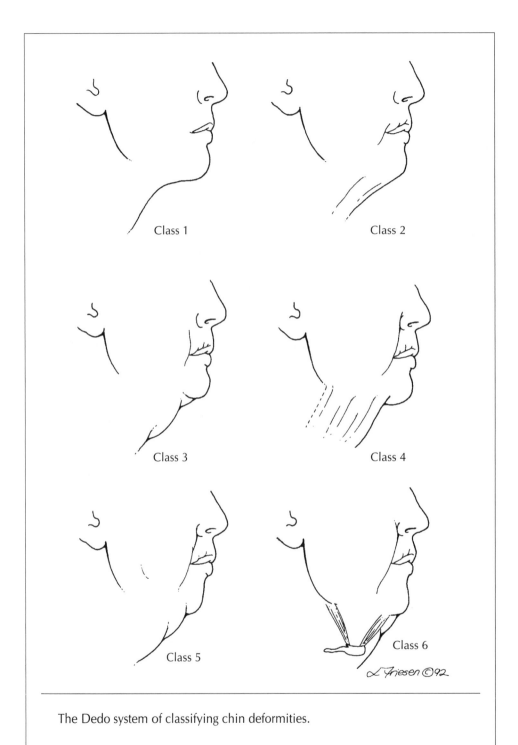

Class 1

Class 2

Class 3

Class 4

Class 5

Class 6

The Dedo system of classifying chin deformities.

Better dental care is the norm these days, so it is rare when we find that neck-chin distortions are the result of dental or skeletal defects, as we do with Class 5 patients. These are people plagued by either congenital or acquired "retrognathia." Their problems of proportion can be caused by an irregular "bite," or imperfect "occlusion" — when the upper and lower teeth don't fit together behind closed lips the way they should. If trouble of this type is identified, a patient will be advised to visit an orthodontist/oral surgeon for assessment and treatment of the bony problem before we start to work on the soft tissue. It is not unusual for a cosmetic surgeon to work closely with an orthodontist or oral surgeon when dealing with problems in this area.

A Class 6 patient is the rare exception to all of Dedo's other classifications: these people have a low-lying "hyoid" bone. The hyoid is the U-shaped bone at the root of your tongue — at the top of your voice box. Quite often, a Class 6 patient appears to have the simpler problems of excessive fat and platysmal cording that we find in other classifications. However, a low-lying hyoid bone is not correctable. Neither oral nor facial plastic surgery will make a difference. However, soft tissue surgery would restore the neck to its more youthful appearance.

Chin Surgery

Analysis of the chin with a normal bite can reveal a chin that is not prominent enough. Further study will tell whether the defect is anterior-posterior prominence from the side view or not enough width (from the front view). Most facial cosmetic surgeons use a wraparound solid silicone implant to correct this. It was designed by my friend, Dr. Harry Mittleman. I use the Mittelman pre-jowl chin implant to create chin projection and chin width, keeping the lower chin area in balance with the rest of the face. They come in different sizes, but can be nicely tailored to individual situations. I make a one-and-a-half centimeter incision under the chin (where twenty percent of people already have a scar through previous trauma, usually a childhood fall). I then elevate the fleshy soft tissue off the bone, creating a pocket for the implant and suturing it in. Infection, mobility, movement, and asymmetry are very rare complications and the patient has a balanced lower third of the face after two weeks.

Analysis of the lower third of the face can also reveal that a patient's chin is much too large in its context. For patients with a normal bite, I can reduce the size of the chin. An incision is made inside and behind the lower lip (below the teeth) to loosen the lip and skin so that we can peel them away to expose the bone underneath. Then we use a surgical vibrating saw to pare down the bone. It's the same sort of saw that a neurosurgeon uses to bore holes in the skull: the saw reacts only to bone, so there is no danger of cutting soft tissue. Afterward, the fleshy part of the chin is restored to its original position with a less prominent chin when the swelling dissipates.

Lip Surgery

Now that you know how we view the lips — as an integral part of the lower third of the face — it might help to look at a few site-specific situations, when only the lips are affected. If the problem involves muscle defects, we'll work on those before doing anything with the soft tissue. As I said in the chapter on linear scarring, sometimes a lip scar will show up when a patient smiles because the muscle hasn't been properly repaired after an accident. We might have to reopen the scar and close the wound with a deep dermal stitch to produce a finer, less visible scar. This is particularly important if scarring mars the vermilion border, making it so noticeable.

If the problem is a paralyzed lower lip, it most often is due to damage to the "ramus mandibularis," the branch of the facial nerve that affects the lip. This nerve gives function to the group of muscles that pulls down or depresses the lower lip. Without this function, people who naturally have a full dental smile suffer the most. When they smile, it looks like a corner of their bottom lip is being pulled by an invisible fish hook because the paralyzed side does not

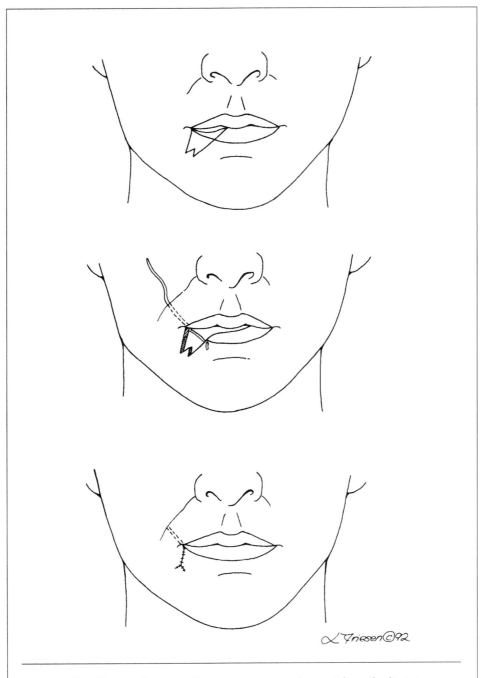

A paralysed lip can be treated by removing a wedge to tighten the lip into a straighter, more horizontal line.

move. But there is an effective technique we can use to almost restore a natural, balanced smile.

We start by cutting out a wedge of the lower lip, which immediately improves the situation by tightening the lip into a straighter horizontal line. (Often, a paralyzed lower lip hangs loosely, due to loss of muscle tone.) This wedge-shaped wound, made near the corner of the mouth, is sewn up with a deeply placed stitch that closes up the muscle to minimize scarring. But before sewing it up, we give the lip a "sling" by suturing it to the groove between the upper lip and the cheek. This exerts a permanent, upward pull that counteracts the slackness in the paralyzed area.

This technique is an exacting form of surgery because it involves a couple of procedures that require experience and some finesse on the part of the surgeon. For example, because the lip is pulled toward the corner of the mouth, the fullest part of the lip moves away from the center of the mouth. As a result, we have to surgically "thin" part of the red segment of the lip so that it looks natural in its new position. And the "sling" itself must be sutured to the muscle of the lip, then slung around the corner of the mouth and attached through an incision to the lip-cheek groove.

Happily, not all patients arrive at a cosmetic surgeon's office in need of such extensive repair work to the lips. Some want to improve the appearance of their lips for cosmetic reasons alone. A fairly typical example is the patient who, as a youngster, got whacked in the mouth by a hockey stick or a set of handlebars in a tricycle accident. This can lead to a scar inside the upper lip, on the lubricating or mucous membrane. The scar thickens and it begins to push down so that a small part of the membrane shows, particularly when the patient smiles. The procedure to correct this is a straightforward excision; we cut out most of the thickened scar and sew up the membrane to produce a finer scar that will heal more evenly.

Young patients who have had surgery to correct the birth deformity of a shortened philtral area, usually referred to as a "harelip," often end up with no tubercle. We can correct this with collagen injections, but a more permanent solution would be to insert a piece of Gore-Tex into the red segment of the upper lip. This would create the appearance of a natural tubercle.

As with any other cosmetic procedure, it is our task to make sure that the limitations of lip surgery are understood. A cosmetic surgeon can work with only the basic equipment a patient brings to the operation; if you have lips as thin as a monkey's ("simian" lips), don't wave a magazine photo of an actress famous for her pout under the surgeon's nose. Thin lips can be made to look fuller than they are to begin with, but simple genetics are a limiting factor. Patients with very full lips, for example, can expect cosmetic surgery to produce lips that are less full — but they likely will never manage to have thin lips. A percentage of my patients are blacks who want an overly protuberant lower lip reduced in size, and again, I have to take the time to explain the limitations of surgery.

A patient's age will also determine what a cosmetic surgeon can reasonably hope to accomplish. I've described previously how the circular muscle surrounding the mouth, the "orbicularis oris," is attached directly to the skin in that area. With age, the muscle shortens, or shrinks a bit, and this causes vertical lines to appear around the lips. This situation can be improved upon with a chemical peel of the upper lip and/or collagen injections every six months to make the lines nearly invisible

Aging might also create problems in the lip area if the patient has had teeth removed over the years. This can result in a loss of bone above the upper teeth, which causes the mouth to "sink" or cave in a little, which in turn, brings down the tip of the nose. In a case like this, I'd be inclined to combine several surgical and nonsurgical techniques to correct the problem: perhaps some rhinoplasty (surgery of the nose) to bring up the tip, along with a chemical peel or collagen injections around the mouth, and maybe even an assessment as to whether a face-lift would help by generally tightening up the lower third of the face.

The Paris Lip

As I mentioned at the beginning of this chapter, some patients are not at all interested in surgical procedures to improve the appearance of their lips; what they want is the extremely popular, nonsurgical procedure of a series of collagen injections. Blame it on pop and movie stars like Barbara Hershey, Julia Roberts and Madonna if you will, but the world is beating a path to the doorways of cosmetic surgeons in search of the luscious lips that one marketing whiz has dubbed "The Paris Lip."

Collagen, as I explained earlier, is a natural product of the dermis layer of human skin. However, The Collagen Corporation of California has two manufactured collagen products on the market called Zyderm, and more recently, Zyplast. Both are injectable biological compositions mixed with anesthetic fluid. Zyderm is used for fine lines around the eyes. Zyplast is a firmer form of collagen used for deeper wrinkles, like frown lines and pronounced lip-cheek grooves. I use Zyplast on the lips of those patients in search of a luscious look.

It's a simple enough procedure. We have the patient settle back into a chair, the same way she would at the dentist's office. (Most, but not all, luscious lip patients are female.) A small mark is made with a felt-tip pen to identify the center of her Cupid's bow, where the red and flesh-colored segments of the upper lip join. We have the patient rub a small amount of topical anesthetic on the mucous membrane just inside her upper lip; it numbs the area and makes the injection more tolerable. Occasionally, we use an injectable anesthetic to make it a totally painless procedure; this causes the area to swell up temporarily.

Even without an injectable anesthetic, the area swells a bit — partly because it's a natural reaction to the puncture of a needle, and partly because collagen contains a small amount (about three percent) of lidocaine.

Lidocaine is a synthetic anesthetic extracted from cocaine. The manufacturers of injectable collagen recognize the need for at least a small amount of local anesthetic so the procedure won't be too painful, but the presence of lidocaine and collagen means each patient must be tested for allergic reaction before undergoing the procedure. We are cautious, too, in injecting patients who have a history of recurrent cold sores on their lips. An injection could acti-

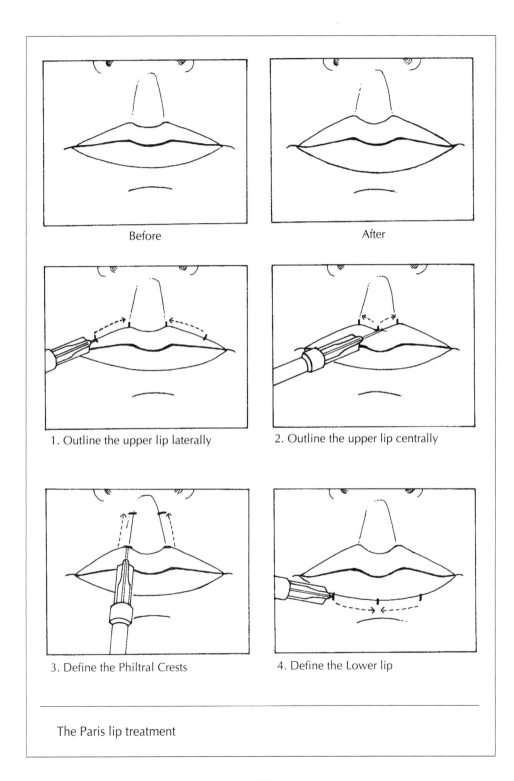

Before

After

1. Outline the upper lip laterally

2. Outline the upper lip centrally

3. Define the Philtral Crests

4. Define the Lower lip

The Paris lip treatment

vate the virus that would cause another sore to develop. Children and women who are pregnant should not have their lips injected, because not enough research has been done to verify whether it is a safe procedure for them.

Once the mark on the Cupid's bow has been made, it will serve as a reference point during the procedure to make sure that the surgeon creates luscious — and symmetrical — lips. The needle is inserted near the commissure, or corner, of one side of the upper lip and collagen is injected in a line that follows exactly the vermilion border. The vermilion border is an excellent site for improving the shape of the Cupid's bow, especially when it is somewhat flat in appearance naturally. The injections raise the bow and "push out" or evert the lip so that it looks fuller. (This could change if a patient has specifically requested injections in the red or flesh-colored segments, depending on what kind of proportion we are trying to achieve in the lips.)

Technique varies from surgeon to surgeon, but I prefer an injection that is neither too near the surface, nor too deep, called linear threading. If the injection is shallow, you can see the line of collagen just below the skin. If it's too deep, it won't be as long-lasting. I slide the tiny needle parallel to the level I want the collagen deposited; it might take two or more injections along the vermilion border to complete one side of the lip. The procedure is repeated on the other side of the upper lip, starting at the top of the Cupid's bow and working down toward the commissure. With each injection, the area affected swells up a bit, so the mark in the middle helps to maintain symmetry even when one side of the lip is swollen and the other side is not.

Injecting collagen into the lips is really "millimeter surgery for millimeter results." Half a cc will generally suffice for a straightforward Paris Lip procedure. Because collagen has a local anesthetic in it, the lips must be over-injected to compensate for the fact that swelling caused by the anesthetic itself will dissipate within twenty-four hours. Some patients want a dramatic look, but I caution against having so much injected that it looks unnatural. (Tell this to Julia Roberts, who seems to like lips that look like cocktail weiners.)

And, for all I've said about it, a tiny bit of asymmetry is not a bad thing; most people have naturally asymmetric features. The injections have to be repeated about every three months, which can vary with the individual, because collagen is a natural substance that dissipates within the body.

Perhaps the best thing about collagen injections to the lips is that the procedure only takes about fifteen minutes, and by the time you get home, most of the reactionary swelling will have disappeared. You can put on your party clothes and go out and show off your new, luscious lips.

CHAPTER EIGHT

The Nose

RHINOPLASTY. ANY GOOD DICTIONARY will crisply define it as "surgery of the nose." The word comes from rhino, the Greek word for nose, and plasto, the Greek word for formed, or molded. It is always a bit of a shock for me to see rhinoplasty reduced to such simple terms, as though you could describe love as a strong predilection, or murder as a deplorable activity. In fact, rhinoplasty is such an emotionally charged area of a cosmetic surgeon's repertoire that it often encompasses love, and occasionally extends to murder.

The Psychology of Rhinoplasty Patients

Dr. Mary Ruth Wright, associate clinical professor of psychology at Baylor College of Medicine in Houston, and a long-time friend of mine, has written some fascinating material on the psychology of patients who undergo rhinoplasty. As I mentioned earlier, Dr. Wright and others have spent years analyzing the psychological significance of the nose. Their conclusion is that the nose is as important as the sexual organs to an individual's self-image or body-image. It makes sense if you look at it in a kind of cursory, clinical way: like the vagina, a nose is an orifice that sometimes emits mucus and has a tendency to bleed; like the penis, a nose undergoes a spurt of growth

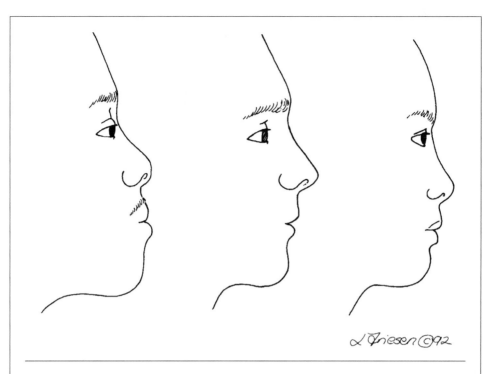

The nose is an important element of an individual's self-image and must be in harmony with the rest of the patient's features.

in adolescence, it contains erectile tissue that can be affected by psychic influences (for example, fear or anger), and it protrudes from the body. This last bit of physical detail, the fact that the nose protrudes, might be the key to understanding why male patients are much more likely than female patients to be upset by the outcome of rhinoplasty. Some psychologists maintain that all features of the human body that are "extended" — such as the penis, fingers, toes, even arms and legs — are the subjects of a deep, subconscious fear that they might be lost, or separated from the body. Hence, a male who subconsciously fears castration might transfer this fear, without understanding it, to his nose. If he is psychotically disturbed, this could elicit an unreasonable rage against his "castrator," the rhinoplastic surgeon.

Female patients, when they are disturbed by rhinoplasty, rarely exhibit this kind of rage. But they do show other signs of deep-seated, subconscious worry. Cosmetic surgeons are warned to watch for the female patient who seems upset by examination with a small nasal speculum (a metal instrument that we use to enlarge and examine the interior of the nose). It could be that she is equating the examination with genital mutilation and it probably would be unwise to proceed with surgery.

Lest you think this identification of the nose with things sexual is farfetched, history shows that the connection has been made for centuries. Ancient Romans believed that the size of the nose accurately indicated the size of the penis, and male adulterers were punished by amputation of the nose. Adulteresses in India were punished the same way for more than a thousand years. Medical historians have noted that we are indebted to the "seminal role played by the abundance of noseless females in India" in the development of the techniques of plastic surgery. And it's no secret that odors detected by insects and animals can affect sexual behavior. Humans who respond to certain perfumes know the attraction of the odor of musk, which is made from the sexual glands of musk deer.

My files contain a few interesting stories with regard to patients who have had trouble dealing with rhinoplasty, despite the fact that I take special care to screen such candidates for surgery. If anything, these stories illustrate how subtle the variations can be on potential problems. For example, there was the time that, at the behest of his wife, I operated on a fellow who had a real bugle of a nose. She was convinced that his nose was causing him all sorts of problems with his self-confidence. I interviewed them together, then separately, and came to the conclusion she was right. The operation to reduce the size of his nose was a success, and this devoted woman spent a lot of her time helping her husband through the preoperative and postoperative process. A couple of years ago, I found out that he'd gained such tremendous self-confidence that he'd left his wife and gone off with another woman to start a new life.

Then there was the woman who came to me for rhinoplasty because she had a rather unattractive wide nose with a bump on the bridge. We did the operation — took the bump off, narrowed the bridge, and narrowed the tip — and away she went, happy, with a much-improved appearance. I should add that this woman was in her early thirties, an intellectual, and that she lived at home with her parents. Almost four years after the operation, she was back in my office: she wanted her nose restored to its original appearance, bump and all. I sent her to a psychiatrist.

In my view, this patient had made a highly unreasonable request, but the psychiatrist came to the conclusion that she was in a "gray" area, meaning, not necessarily psychologically upset, and that we could probably safely proceed with the restorative operation. After about ten consultations with her, I finally agreed to do the work. The day of the operation, early in the morning, she was sitting in the patient holding area — dressed in a hospital gown — when she changed her mind. Decided against the operation, just like that. To this day, I don't really know what happened to cause this patient such anguish, though I suspect that perhaps her parents had been exerting some kind of influence.

Dr. Wright has cited studies that show "type-changing" rhinoplasty is much less acceptable to older patients than it is to younger patients. At least one cosmetic surgeon has stated that he will no longer perform such surgery on patients older than thirty-five. "Type-changing" rhinoplasty is elective surgery (surgery entered into by choice) that actually alters the appearance of a patient's face. Younger people, maybe because they are more open to change in general, are usually happy with the results of a rhinoplasty that makes a noticeable difference. Older people have a more firmly entrenched idea of who they are, based on what they look like. A change in their appearance sometimes causes a loss of identity. This phenomenon could be what was troubling my patient; perhaps her parents reacted to her altered appearance with altered behavior and she wanted to get her "old self" back.

Two other stories from my files serve to illustrate the complex reactions that rhinoplasty can incite, especially in male patients. The first involves a patient who was seventeen years old when I operated on him. He had seemed reasonable in consultation and knew exactly what he wanted: the width of his nose narrowed and the "dorsum," or bridge, built up a bit. One year after the operation, he was on the telephone, very abusive to my secretaries, and upset about the work done. But when he came in to see me, he was remarkably polite and I suggested that perhaps he should see a psychiatrist before undergoing any revisional surgery. Soon enough, he was back on the phone, more abusive than before. The personal threats of death became serious, so we had him arrested, and he ended up in an infirmary for a while. Two years later, he showed up again in my office, for a nice, reasonable chat about possible revisions to his nose. "I don't think I can help you," is all I said. Something tells me this isn't the end of the story; time will tell.

The second story is a classic illustration of the perfectionist, though in this case, he ended up going a little bonkers. This fellow had had several operations on his nose by the time he came to me. He wanted me to open up his nose and remove some of the cumulative scarring inside. I put him through a number of tests, and collected all of the operative notes from the other surgeons. I came to

Anatomy of the outside of the nose

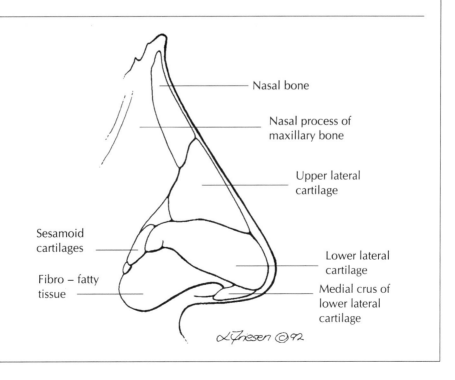

Nasal bone

Nasal process of maxillary bone

Upper lateral cartilage

Sesamoid cartilages

Fibro – fatty tissue

Lower lateral cartilage

Medial crus of lower lateral cartilage

the conclusion that he would need laser treatment to break down the scars and gave him the name of a surgeon who had the proper equipment. Within a week, he had taken a shotgun into his previous surgeon's office and discharged it into the ceiling. Then he burned his girlfriend's house to the ground.

Expectations

I'm sure by now you must be wondering why on earth a cosmetic surgeon is at all willing to perform the rhinoplasty procedure. Well, for one thing, the level of dissatisfaction following a rhinoplasty can range from the sensational stories I've related above to a transient depression lasting a couple of days after the operation (mostly due to the patient's reaction to an unwholesome, bruised appearance during the early stages of healing). So not everyone is out for revenge with a shotgun, and modern preoperative counseling has been enormously helpful in weeding out the truly disturbed candidate.

Something else to consider is the fact that a huge number of rhinoplasties are performed every year. Consequently, even a small percentage of dissatisfied patients translates into a seemingly high number. Rhinoplasty is the most popular facial plastic surgery procedure, followed by eye surgery. In Ontario alone, where I practice, I would estimate that over 15,000 rhinoplasties have been performed within the past five years. (Roughly double the amount covered by the provincial health care plan.) Of these, perhaps 2,000 patients are dissatisfied with their results, to one degree or another.

The truth about rhinoplasties, however, is that they are practically irresistible for the surgeon, no matter the risks. They incorporate all of the things that a cosmetic surgeon loves most: aesthetic judgment, technical complexity and challenge. Without question, a rhinoplasty is the most difficult of all cosmetic operations to perform. There are at least fifty-five different maneuvers that can be applied to the nose, and the combination of ways to use them is as unlimited as the variety of work to be done. The nose is the true Rubik's Cube of cosmetic surgery; it can be rearranged from side to side, up and down, and back and forth.

To give you an idea of just how fascinating rhinoplasty is, I'll tell you a tale straight out of the 1960s, when things were different and almost every medical resident at the University of Toronto was a guy. For four years, we met across the street for a beer or two after grueling days of training and practice. Each year, there were special courses devoted to training in rhinoplasty and whenever those courses were conducted, we'd come out of the pub and realize that all we could remember about the gorgeous woman at the bar was what her nose looked like. This might not mean a lot to female medical residents, but for us, in those days, our fixation was a revelation.

The technical complexity of rhinoplasty is something that can be mastered with continual training and time and assessment of the results, but aesthetic judgment is another matter. Patients sometimes ask if there is a kind of "universal" nose, a nose for all time that will forever be fashionable. I suspect they might be thinking about the turned-up "French" nose that was popular in Hollywood when cosmetic surgery began to gain acceptance in the late 1960s and early 1970s. It may have been a fashionable nose in Hollywood, but I would quickly have gone out of business if I'd tried to impose it on my clientele, then largely Italian-Canadians and other people of Mediterranean extraction. This is the first lesson of aesthetic judgment: make the nose fit the genetic background. Don't give a cute button nose to an Italian male, unless you're looking for trouble.

Height is another basic aesthetic consideration when it comes to rhinoplasty. I've had patients who are six feet tall come into my office, looking for a shortened nose. A shorter nose is generally more upturned, and my first question is: "Would it bother you if your next date spent the whole evening looking up your nose?" That's exactly what would happen, of course; the tall patient must be counseled to consider the overall harmony of body shape and facial features.

Roughly speaking, harmony exists in the face if it can be divided into equal thirds from the hairline to the top of the brows, from the brows to the bottom of the nose, from the nose to the bottom of the chin. Within each of these thirds, there are other, measurable equations to determine if facial features like the eyes, nostrils and lips are

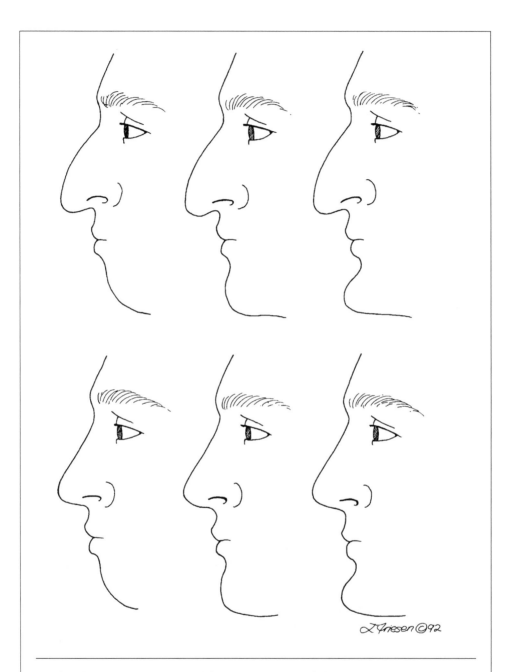

The chin is an integral part of facial harmony (or disharmony) and must be considered when nose surgery is planned. Both the large and averaged sized noses above are affected by small, average or over-sized chins.

evenly distributed. Overall, a harmonious blend of features should produce a balanced, pleasing profile.

The nose is one of the most important parts of a good profile. Most of the people who approach a cosmetic surgeon for rhinoplastic work have come to the conclusion that their nose does not harmonize with the rest of their face: it is upsetting the balance of features. Perhaps the nose is too big, or too small or misshapen in some way. Only some of them have taken into account how the nose is affecting their profile. I suppose this is partly because most people don't bother with a three-way mirror in the bedroom or the bathroom. All they are concerned with is the view that others have of them face-to-face. Some are shocked when they initially see their face in profile, or in a profile photograph. But the first thing that a cosmetic surgeon will do is analyze the profile. A profile reveals how balance will ultimately be achieved.

On profile, the nose, chin, lips and forehead are the key features. If the chin is "weak," or what we call "retrodisplaced" (meaning, backward from its usual place), a well-proportioned nose, even after cosmetic surgery, will not solve the problem of facial disharmony. It could be that further work is needed by an orthodontist or an oral surgeon to correct problems of bite alignment. Or a cosmetic surgeon might be able to balance the chin by bringing it forward visually. This can be done, simply enough with a bit of "mentoplasty."

"Mentoplasty" (from *mentum*, the Latin word for chin), usually involves an implant underneath the soft tissues of the chin, next to the bone. The pocket it sits in within the soft tissues holds it in place. This implant is made from medical-grade solid plastic called Sialastic and it looks like something you might find in a fisherman's lure box, a flexible, sinewy strip of plastic that is wider in the middle and tapered to either end, like the shape of the rind on a wedge of lemon. It is slightly hollowed on the inside so that it cups the chinbone perfectly. A cosmetic surgeon has a variety of implants to choose from, depending on the existing shape of a patient's chin.

Chin augmentation adds only about half an hour to a rhinoplasty operation, and it can make all the difference in the world. Likewise, a too-large chin can be corrected by removing excessive bone. Or the profile might be improved by liposuction; vacuuming out excess fat to eliminate a double chin. At least one-quarter of the patients who arrive at a cosmetic surgeon's office looking for a rhinoplasty would benefit greatly from another, secondary form of profile work as well.

The frustrating thing is that often patients cannot be convinced of the value of a chin implant or other technique. They remain totally focused on their nose and don't understand that part of the problem stems from the chin, or one of the other profile features. As a result, a rhinoplasty can be disappointing; the surgeon knows full well that the job could be better done. It's especially upsetting if the new, perfectly balanced nose ends up making the secondary problem even more apparent.

With regard to the nose itself, there are many interesting variations on what a cosmetic surgeon might be asked to correct. I've had families bring in their children because the combination of features between a husband and wife has produced genetic restructuring that is aesthetically unpleasing. For example, the husband might have a magnificent nose that suits his large face perfectly, and the wife might have a delicate little chin that suits her face. Together, they have produced a child with a big nose and a tiny chin: a rhinoplastic challenge.

Another common scenario is when parents bring in a young child who has suffered a nasal injury. The accident might have been a long time ago: I've seen a child up to three years after an injury, when his nose appeared to be growing in an odd shape, even though the accident itself hadn't resulted in any fractures. The cartilage of the nose was injured at the time of the accident, so it stopped growing. The bone, however, continued to grow. When the doctor who saw the child after the accident took X-rays, only the bone was revealed and it showed no damage. (Cartilage doesn't show up on an X-ray.) Often, the family is amazed when I point out the cartilage, which may have bowed out into an airway. This same problem often causes breathing problems in young children.

Careful palpation — feeling with the fingers — of the framework of the nose and its envelope of skin is an important part of the preparatory work before a rhinoplasty operation. Fingers are a cosmetic surgeon's antennae. They relay vital information about the upper and lower cartilages, the septum (a membrane inside the nose that separates the nostrils), the nasal bones, the premaxilla bones that connect to the upper jaw, and the skin inside and overlying the nose. Palpation would reveal a great deal about the extent of the problem with cartilage in a child's nose, for example.

Initial Surgery

Making the Nose Smaller

The number and type of rhinoplasty operations are as various as the people who want them. I'll explain a couple of the more popular requests for rhinoplasty, but these are by no means representative of the entire spectrum of nasal plastic surgery.

The insertion of a chin implant like one of the ones shown below can make the difference between a successful rhinoplasty and one that is disappointing.

(PHOTO COURTESY OF McGHAN MEDICAL CORPORATION)

The most common request for rhinoplasty comes from people who want their nose made smaller and a bump on the bridge removed at the same time. This involves utilizing three or four of the fifty-five possible maneuvers I could do. For one, the tip of the nose will be "dropped" by surgically adjusting the parts of the nose that support the tip. This allows the tip to descend slightly, making the nose appear smaller. Once this is done, the nasal profile is checked and adjusted if necessary so that it remains straight.

To remove the bump, which is made up of an excess of cartilage and bone on the dorsum, we open up the nose to remove the excess with a hammer and chisel, and specialized cartilage shears. Once the bump is gone, the "nasal pyramid" must be reconstructed. The "pyramid" is the overall shape of the bridge of the nose as it relates to the cheeks. Reconstruction involves fracturing the nasal bones where they attach to the cheeks, then setting them to reconstitute the bony and cartilaginous "pyramid."

Any number of tip-narrowing techniques can be employed to make a nose look smaller, depending on the size of the tip to begin with and its relation to the rest of the nose. Most often, a patient will initiate surgery by complaining of the tip that looks "boxy" — square-shaped and fleshy. It is rare that simple tip narrowing will solve the problem; usually I combine this maneuver with others to achieve the best result.

Finally, facial plastic surgery can be used to make a nose look smaller by "shortening" a long nose. The nose might appear to be too long only in relation to the rest of the patient's face. More likely, however, the nose looks long because the angle between the upper lip and the columella is less than ninety degrees. (The columella is the cartilage and soft tissue that divide the nostrils from the tip of the nose to the top of the philtrum.) When this angle is raised, it looks like the nose has been "shortened," which leaves the impression that it is smaller. A rule of thumb is that surgeons try to give women an angle of about 110 to 120 degrees; men look best with an angle between 90 and 110 degrees.

Saddle Nose

Another fairly common request is for surgery to correct what we call "saddle nose deformity." This is a somewhat dramatic phrase that describes the nose with a concave bridge. The "saddle" is the part of the bridge, or dorsum, that lacks enough bone and/or cartilage to allow the nose a proper vault. Often the tip of the nose is normal, which serves to accentuate the problem.

The two main causes of saddle nose are heredity and trauma. Trauma means the cause was an accident of some sort, leading to a loss of some of the bone or cartilage from the dorsum of the nose. Trauma often results in a functional problem as well as a cosmetic problem; the septum might have collapsed, causing difficulty with breathing.

As for heredity, any family can pass along a ski-jump, but broadly speaking, blacks and Orientals seek out cosmetic surgery more often than other races to refine the natural "saddle" shape of their nose.

Saddle nose

This is not to say, by the way, that they want a drasticallly changed nose that looks Caucasian (most are aware of and not impressed by rock star Michael Jackson's transformation). Rather, they want a nose that is more harmonious with the rest of their face. This often involves building up the dorsum and reducing the size of the nasal base, and/or the tip.

Once the surgeon has made a basic assessment of the problem — looking for breathing problems and determining the severity of the "saddle," or depression — he will be able to decide which materials to use to build up the dorsum. This depends on whether the depression has been caused by a lack of bone, a lack of cartilage, or both. The general rule is to use like material to replace missing matter. For example, a cartilaginous depression is corrected with a cartilaginous transplant rather than by bone. Bone would give an unnatural feeling to the nose by being hard and stiff in a normally pliant area.

If the problem is a lack of cartilage, I favor taking a transplant from the patient's own nose to create the "three-dimensional volume filler" that I need. This is an expression we use to describe material that must correct depth, width and height at the same time — as opposed to skin, for example, which is a two-dimensional material not expected to correct problems of depth, or depression. I can only use the patient's own nasal cartilage if the "saddle" is shallow enough that we need only a small amount.

If the depression is deep and I need extra cartilage, I will harvest it from the patient's ears. Specifically, it is conchal ear cartilage that works well as a nasal volume filler. The conchal part of the ear is the internal "cup" above the lobe; the cartilage can be harvested from behind the ear so that no scarring shows. In rare cases when there is not enough combined cartilage for the job in the patient's own nose and ears, and, if there is a need for bone filler as well, we can harvest what we need from the patient's hip. Unfortunately, this is a rather painful procedure and the patient may have to walk with a cane for a week afterward.

It can be upsetting to look in the mirror after an operation to correct a saddle nose deformity: often the nose looks noticeably larger. This is partly because it takes a while to get used to a new nose, but

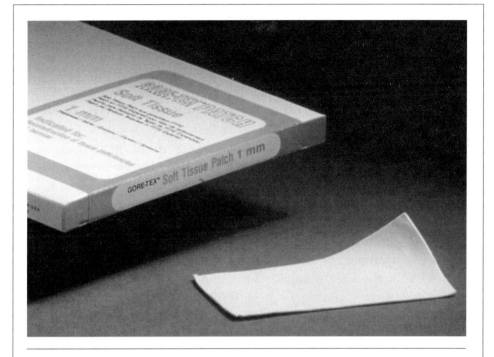

Solid implants for the nose are now made of a synthetic materials like Gore-Tex (above). (PHOTO COURTESY OF W.L. GORE & ASSOCIATES INC.)

also because it is wise for a surgeon to overcompensate during this procedure. Cartilage and bone have a tendency to absorb into the body as they "take" or graft during healing. After two years, only eighty to ninety percent of the originally transplanted material is likely to remain. As a result, the amount of filler used should exceed 100 percent of what is needed at the time of the operation.

The scenarios I've described above apply to the more severe cases of saddle nose deformity. If the cause of the depression is heredity, the problem is usually more minor in nature. The patient might need only a small amount of augmentation, in which case we can use a medical-grade implant instead of harvesting material from another part of the body.

In the early 1960s, medical-grade implants for the nose were made from solid Sialastic plastic, and sometimes they gave us some trouble. Sialastics extruded through the nasal skin after cosmetic surgery. As a resident, I saw this happen often enough. The problem was that Sialastics in the dorsum of the nose were too rigid — eventually, the natural movement of the nose caused them to poke through the skin. Today we use hugely improved medical-grade implants for the nose made from a synthetic material called Medpor, which closely resembles natural bone in composition. The implants remind me of the material used to make Styrofoam coffee cups; it is white and porous and feels similarly dry and slightly rough to the touch. Medpor actually allows the patient's flesh to "in-grow," or meld with the implant as it heals. (Another implant is Gore-Tex, which is soft and pliable.) This allows for flexibility in the nose where it should naturally be, and hence the risk of extrusion has been all but eliminated.

As with the chin, implants for the nose come in a variety of shapes and sizes, and they can be further shaped to suit the exact needs of any patient with a saddle nose.

Columella Deformity

Another request for rhinoplasty comes from patients with what we call "nasal columella deformity." There is usually more to the columella than meets the eye: it widens near the base and inside the nostrils to connect with muscles that allow it to tense the septum (a membrane inside the nose between the two nostrils) and give it the strength to help support the nasal tip. I specify "usually" more than meets the eye because people with the deformity of a hanging columella show much more of the inside of their nose than they want to.

In a paper presented to the American Academy of Facial Plastic and Reconstructive Surgery, Dr. Jerry J. Halik and I outlined the properties of what might be called the ideal columella. Ordinarily, the two "wings" of the nostrils, known as the "alae," should be parallel to the line of the columella, creating evenly spaced nostrils. The angle created by the columella and the protruding upper lip should be greater than ninety degrees. The base of the columella should not project out too far, and the upper lip shouldn't be too short by comparison. Ideally, the columella should, on profile, hang lower than the "alae" by about four millimeters. With a hanging columella deformity, it droops much further. On profile, this can give the appearance of very large, open nostrils.

There are a couple of ways to deal with a hanging columella. The least surgically intensive method is to trim away some of the septum so that less of it is exposed. This won't work, of course, unless the septum is too long in the first place. The second method is to trim back the "medial crura" — the area where the columella flares out at the bottom to create two saucerlike depressions inside the base of the nose — if they are particularly wide.

There are other problems to do with columella deformities: patients with too wide a columellar base, others with a retracted columella, or a short columella, and those with no columella. As I mentioned earlier, the variety of rhinoplastic procedures is as wide-ranging as the patients

A hanging columella can be corrected through surgery.

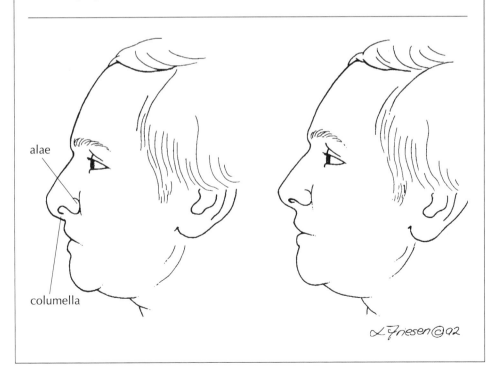

who seek treatment. There are at least ten techniques for lengthening the short columella alone.

Revisional Treatment

The most challenging task a cosmetic surgeon can be presented with is revisional rhinoplasty: operating on a patient who has already had one or more nose jobs. For a variety of reasons the rate of patient dissatisfaction with rhinoplasty can run as high as thirty percent. This represents a large pool of potential patients for an enterprising surgeon, but there is good reason to be cautious.

Again, the motives and psychological makeup of the dissatisfied patient must be carefully assessed before any work is done, but more than that, revisional rhinoplasty requires that the surgeon have tremendous confidence that the problems are actually correctable. Primary rhinoplasty is the most complex of all aesthetic surgical procedures; revisional rhinoplasty multiplies the complexity.

There are two types of patients that most cosmetic surgeons will avoid treating with revisional rhinoplasty: the perfectionist, and the patient who is vague about what exactly seems to be wrong with the nose. Sometimes the latter group will describe the new nose as "ugly" without giving any particular reason why. Both types seem unable to comprehend that cosmetic surgery improves so-called "deformities" but rarely corrects them 100 percent.

I can recall one candidate for revisional rhinoplasty who came to see me because he'd had a nose job done elsewhere, but found that the grooves at the bottom of his nostrils were not exactly the same. During the facial assessment, I took a measurement and found the grooves differed by one millimeter. The chances are good that if I'd gone ahead to try to correct a one-millimeter problem, I might have ended up creating a two-millimeter problem. Ours is not an exact art.

In a paper I presented to the American Academy of Facial Plastic and Reconstructive Surgery with Dr. K. Thomas Robbins and Dr. A.M. Rubin, we drew attention to the fact that any patient undergoing revisional rhinoplasty should understand that there is a possibility of making the nose worse. This is called the "downside risk." Things can go wrong when the patient's original nose had a "twist" of some sort in the nasal dorsum, either in the bone or the cartilage, which has disappeared with the initial rhinoplastic surgery. This "twist" might reappear with revisional rhinoplasty, as though the nose had a memory for it. It's an outcome almost impossible to predict.

The preparatory work involved in revisional rhinoplasty is extensive, at least on the part of the surgeon. Operative notes should be collected from the patient's previous surgeon, or surgeons, if possible. I say this with some hesitation because I've found that the notes are often of little value; it's very difficult for most surgeons to put into words the exact changes in the cartilage and bone they made during each complex, technical step. The most valuable record a patient can provide is a photograph of the original nose. Studying the photograph and comparing it to the patient in person is extremely helpful to a surgeon planning revisional work.

Palpation tells the story about previous work done: whether a surgeon might have incorrectly performed one of the myriad steps involved in rhinoplasty, or whether he skipped a step or, perhaps, over- or under-estimated the amount of work that had to be done in the first place.

A visual inspection of the nose reveals important basic information about skin thickness, pigmentation and scarring. But the patient may also undergo testing for the possible presence of nasal, sinus or biochemical disease like allergies or infections. Patients who wear glasses present a special case; it has to be taken into account exactly where the spectacles fit on the nasal dorsum. (Glasses can affect the healing process by applying pressure on the recently fractured nasal bones, narrowing the vault too much. Patients should wait four weeks after the operation before wearing eyeglasses on the nose. It may be necessary to tape glasses to the forehead if the patient really can't see without them or is unable to wear contact lenses.)

A final point to consider before launching into revisional rhinoplasty is the amount of time that has passed since the previous operation. No major revisional surgery should be undertaken before six months have gone by and I usually like to wait a year. This is because rhinoplasty allows a patient to be up and around and back at work within a couple of weeks, but the true healing process takes a year or more. Problems that arise shortly after surgery might settle in and correct themselves after healing. I have treated at least one patient whose nose took three years to fully heal and stabilize — due to extraordinarily thick skin — before we could start revisional work.

In the twenty years that I have been practicing, it seems to me that most revisional rhinoplasty centers around several basic dynamic (movable) parts of the nose: the relationship between the tip of the nose and its underside, and the relationship between the tip of the nose and the nasal dorsum. In other words, the relationship between the tip and various parts of the nose that support it.

As well, I've found that revisional work tends to fall into fairly predictable categories. People want the tip of their nose narrowed, or the "nasal base" narrowed — the area at the base of the nose extending across the width of the nostrils. Or they want the angle from the tip of the nose to the base of the nostrils made more acute, which as I explained is sometimes part of the technique to "shorten" the nose. Again, with regard to the tip, many patients want it to project out further, or they want it brought back toward the face a bit.

There are two ways to go about operating on the nose, whether it's primary or revisional rhinoplasty. A surgeon can "open up" the nose by making a small incision across the columella and around the nostrils so that the soft tissue can be flipped back to reveal the structure of bone and cartilage underneath. Or the surgeon can take the "endonasal" approach. Endo is derived from the Greek word meaning "within"; the entire operation is conducted more or less out of sight as the surgeon works through the orifices of the nostrils.

Revisional surgery can be done endonasally, but in certain cases, the nose must be opened up even though it's a more surgically intensive operation. This would happen, for example, if the surgeon hadn't been able to determine exactly what went wrong with previous operation(s). For example, there may be a "twist" in the nasal dorsum. Or it would be necessary to open up the nose if any grafting of bone or cartilage had to be done. Sometimes, if excess scarring is to be removed, it requires this approach. I find, too, that if the patient is having trouble with a grossly asymmetrical nasal tip (due to uneven distribution of the cartilage), that I have to open up the nose to fix it.

Generally speaking, a surgeon has to make use of a wider variety of techniques for revisional rhinoplasty than might be necessary for primary surgery. But overall, the guiding principle is to inflict as little surgery as possible. For one, this reduces the likelihood that previously corrected problems will reappear. For another, limited surgery translates into less swelling after the operation, and less swelling means the patient will heal more quickly.

Recovery

After rhinoplasty, a patient can expect to suffer swelling and discoloration around the nose and eyes, but very little pain. In a survey of my own patients, I found that twenty-five percent took no pain medication at all. Any pain can usually be handled with Tylenol 3, available by prescription.

Surgeons will place a small cast on the nose after rhinoplasty. The purpose of the cast is not to hold the nasal bones in position, but rather to reduce swelling around the surgical field. The cast is usually removed during the first postoperative visit.

Bruising around the eyes is often worse the second day after the operation. Most of it is gone within two weeks, but in the meantime, sleeping with your head propped up will help to minimize the discomfort: swelling is affected by gravity, so the more time you spend upright, especially at night, the faster it will clear. Avoid lifting, bending or any activity that would increase body temperature or blood pressure. As the swelling subsides, the discoloration will become more noticeable; first dark, then a yellowish hue, before it fades away. This is perfectly normal, and those who are comfortable with cosmetics can conceal discoloration reasonably well. A trip to an aesthetician specializing in cosmetic camouflage techniques can be helpful for this sort of bruising.

There is as much swelling inside your nose as there is outside, and this will result in nasal blockage. You'll have to breathe through your

mouth until it subsides, so make sure you've got a ready supply of fluids, hard candies and mouthwash at hand. The dry mouth will go away
after about two weeks, when the swelling is gone.

As long as you've avoided strenuous activity, there shouldn't be any
fresh bleeding from the nose, but you can expect a blood-tinged discharge for the first week. It's important to wear a "mustache" dressing
to catch these secretions, because any dabbing or wiping might affect
the cosmetic and/or functional outcome of the operation. Don't be
tempted to use over-the-counter vaso-constrictive sprays like Otrivin or
Neo-Synephrine to help clear the nose. If the discharge is particularly
thick and bothersome, mix 5 mL (one teaspoon) of salt into 500 mL
(two cups) of water to make a solution, then squeeze a few drops at a
time into the nostrils, using an eyedropper. This will help to liquefy the
secretions and break up any crust that might form after the first week.

Once the discharge has stopped, crusting will naturally occur. Do

A small cast is usually placed on the nose after rhinoplasty to reduce the
swelling caused by the operation.

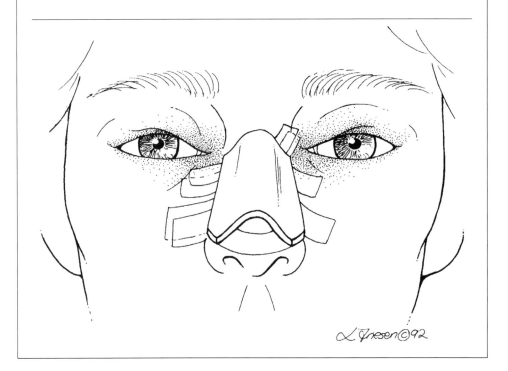

146

not, under any circumstances, pick inside your nose to remove crusts. Picking might lead to further bleeding and abnormal healing. Instead, use Q-tips soaked in a solution of three percent hydrogen peroxide, or Q-tips dipped in a small amount of Polysporin ointment, to soften the crusting so that the scabs will fall away. If a crust is very adherent and won't come away, leave it alone for another day or two, but don't pick.

In the unfortunate event that a nosebleed does develop, fill a plastic bag with ice chips and rest it gently on the bridge of your nose for fifteen minutes. If this doesn't stop it, go straight to your doctor, or the hospital.

If the rhinoplasty you've had done involved surgery at the base of the nose, below the nostrils, your upper lip will be stiff after the operation. This will give you a rather strange smile. Again, this is due to swelling and you'll get your normal smile back in about two weeks. In the meantime, avoid pursing your lips or kissing for the first week, and if you must wear lipstick, put it on gently with a brush. Be extremely careful not to hurt the tissues of the upper lip if you decide to brush your teeth. If brushing is at all painful, stop.

As I mentioned earlier in this chapter, people who wear eyeglasses are at a disadvantage after rhinoplasty. Glasses should not be worn for four weeks after an operation because there is a good chance they might affect, or distort, the nasal bones as they heal. Tape the lenses to your forehead if you must have them to see. Patients who wear contact lenses are luckier — they can usually be worn within two days after surgery.

As for personal grooming, try to rough it for a couple of days. You can, very gently, wash your face, but you should not wash your hair until the cast is removed — usually within a week. You should also avoid hot water and hair dryers for a full two weeks following surgery as the heat might aggravate the swelling. (If the situation is desperate, use a dry shampoo.) Don't pluck your eyebrows for two weeks following surgery and expect to suffer oily skin on your nose and mid-face area for a month after the operation. After the cast is off, you can begin to use light astringents or glycolic acid creams or lotions on your face to prevent infection from pimples.

Treat your nose with enormous respect for two weeks following surgery — don't even try to slip a T-shirt or a sweater over your head unless the neck hole is wide enough to ensure that you won't bump your nose while dressing or undressing. It will take four weeks before your nose can withstand even moderate stress or trauma. If you take a hard blow to the nose during this time, report it immediately to your surgeon. If you like sports where the chances of getting hit on the nose are high, like basketball or high diving, quell your passion for a full four months.

If this advice for conduct during the healing process after rhinoplasty seems unduly restrictive, the reason may now be clear. Primary rhinoplasty is the most complex of all aesthetic surgical procedures; revisional rhinoplasty on a botched or improperly healed nose operation multiplies the complexity. And you might have to wait one or more years for the primary surgery to fully heal.

The Ears

IN 1941, WALT DISNEY PRODUCTIONS released a movie about a baby elephant called Dumbo. Dumbo was dropped off by Ol' Doc Stork at a circus, and the more experienced Big Top elephants didn't think much of this clumsy little newcomer with the huge ears. Eventually, Dumbo learned that he had a special talent: his ears were so big he could fly! At the end of the movie, Dumbo became a hero and the entire circus celebrated him with a parade. But most of the story was about Dumbo's misadventures — he was always getting into trouble — and the lasting impression was that the little elephant with the big ears was, well, dumb. Unintelligent. Stupid.

From the moment of Dumbo's release, every kid on the block with big ears, or "flyaway" ears as they are sometimes called, became the target of name-calling by neighborhood bullies. It's an unfortunate characteristic of our society that outstanding physical features can make a kid the brunt of such teasing. Whenever I see a young patient with flyaway ears, I remember the movie and reflect on this rite of passage. I like to think that most of these boys and girls will grow up to do something special, just like Dumbo, but in the meantime, there is something I can do for them.

Otoplasty, plastic surgery of the ear, can be performed on kids as young as four or five, just about the time they are entering kinder-

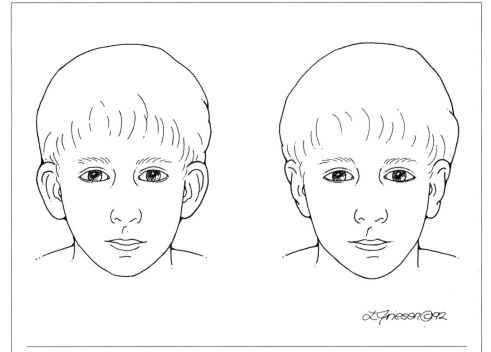

Flyaway ears can be corrected through surgery, and patients can be as young as four or five years old.

garten or grade school. There are many reasons for performing cosmetic ear surgery: some people are born without an ear, or only part of an ear; some lose part of an ear in an accident; others have ears that are too big for their heads; and some babies are born with "lop" ears that fold over on themselves. In this chapter, however, I'd like to concentrate on the procedure that I am most often asked for: otoplasty to correct flyaway ears.

Otoplasty at a young age spares kids the humiliation of being teased throughout the formative years of public and junior high school. There are some who will say that teasing is a part of character-building, but I am of the opinion that there are plenty of other, more constructive things going on during these years that will build a child's character. In fact, constant teasing about looks sometimes has the opposite effect and destroys a child's self-confidence, with unpleasant ramifications for adult life. In most parts of

Canada, the operation is covered by provincial health insurance up to the age of eighteen.

Unlike the nose, where we have to delay the cosmetic operation until it has stopped growing, usually until about age fifteen or sixteen, the ears have more or less reached maturity by age five. There is research that suggests ears never stop growing, but continue to grow very, very slowly throughout life. If it's true, then the rate of growth is slowest after age five.

Most of my otoplasty patients are the young set, but every year I get a number of patients with flyaway ears who are older, eighteen years and more. Most say they are tired of wearing their hair in a style that conceals their ears. Or they didn't realize when they were younger that it was such a relatively simple operation. Otoplasty is, in fact, one of the less complex operations performed by facial cosmetic surgeons. It takes only an hour and a half to do, and adults can usually get by with a local anesthetic and a little sedation. Children require a general anesthetic, but they can be discharged from hospital the same day of surgery.

Flyaway Ears

The ear is an organ that controls balance as well as hearing. It is composed of three parts: the inner ear, middle ear and outer ear. The auditory nerve in the inner ear, that part of the ear nearest to the brain, transmits hearing signals to the appropriate parts of the brain through tiny parts called the "cochlea." The middle ear contains the delicate bones named for their shapes — the "hammer," "anvil" and "stirrup" — which collect information about what we hear and pass it on to the cochlea of the inner ear. The middle ear also contains the "eustachian tube," which is connected to the nasal cavity and acts to equalize air pressure on the inside of the eardrum with pressure outside. The eardrum itself, a thin membrane, separates the middle ear from the outer ear. It is the outer ear that we operate on with an otoplasty for flyaway ears.

The outer ear has several distinct parts, most of which are designed to collect sound waves and funnel them into the middle ear through the ear canal. The deepest part of this canal is the only part of the outer ear that is not visible to the eye. The parts of the outer ear that are visible — the folds of skin and cartilage known as the "pinna" — are the cosmetically important areas that otoplasty can improve.

There are three basic components to the phenomenon of flyaway ears. First, there is the "anti-helical fold," which is the crease in the visible part of the ear just under the outer rim, which is called the "helix." The fold causes the "helix" to curve inward at the top of the ear. Without the fold, the ear stands out from the head; it "flies away." Some people are born without the anti-helical fold; it usually is a genetic defect, passed through generations of a family even if it skips a generation or two. Second, associated with this unfurling of the fold, the earlobe, or "lobule" as it is called, might extend from the head horizontally, instead of hanging down as it should. Third, the "conchal bowl," the bowl-like depression in the middle of the

Anatomy of the ear

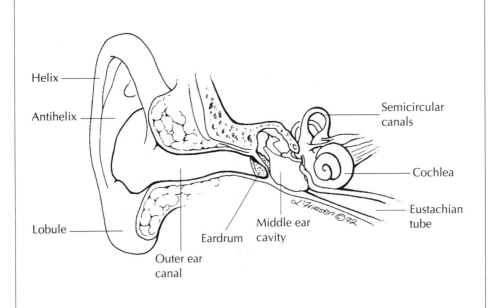

outer ear, might be too big. Technically, the bowl is actually too wide, and its width causes the ear to push out, or rotate away from the head. None of these physical characteristics affect hearing; neither does an operation to correct flyaway ears.

Normally, ears protrude from the head by about fifteen to twenty millimeters. Flyaway ears stick out further, sometimes a little, sometimes a lot. It is not unusual to treat a patient with only one flyaway ear or ears that stick out at different degrees. The thing to remember is that no two ears are exactly the same even on the well-proportioned person with no need for otoplasty. Some of my adult patients need counseling before otoplasty to fully understand that it is not an exact art and that their ears still might not be identical after surgery. Usually, I can make my case by pointing out the differences that already exist in their ears. Most earlobes, for example, are at different heights. If all else fails, I'll show them the evidence of my own ears, my secretaries' ears and assistant's ears: no two ears are the same on any one head.

We start the procedure, then, with an analysis of the degree to which the anti-helical fold has unfurled, the depth of the conchal bowl and the plane of the lobule. During the analysis, the cartilage of the outer ear is checked for its quality, or "spring." (You can check your own ears for this by flipping the pinnae forward: if they spring back into position, the quality of your cartilage is elastic or springy.) Cartilaginous quality will dictate some of the suturing technique in the last part of the otoplasty; a too springy ear may require more stitches or surgical techniques to weaken the cartilage a bit. In children, the cartilage is less springy, which makes their ears more amenable to correction.

What we are trying to accomplish with an otoplasty is to create a natural angle between the ear and the head. If it's missing, we also want to create an anti-helical fold that looks as natural as possible. And we'll aim for angling the lobule so that it's on the same plane as the anti-helical fold. If you take a look at yourself in the mirror, you'll see that your lobules, or earlobes, are on the same angle as the upper part of the ear; they don't, or shouldn't, stick out independently. You might also notice that it's important that they are as evenly proportioned as possible from the face-to-face view. Try pulling one lower than the other — it makes your face look a bit off-kilter.

Surgery

The technique I've developed for operating on flyaway ears has evolved into nine basic steps. Step one is to make an incision through the skin at the back of the ear about ten millimeters behind the helical rim. This is the first of two cuts that will eventually produce a rectangular-shaped flap of tissue to be flipped open.

Step two is to raise the skin and soft tissue behind the ear to expose the cartilage underneath. The cartilage is still attached to its covering membrane, known as the "perichondrium." The dissection is carried along the entire vertical length of the helical rim, and further down toward the lobule if the patient also has the problem of protruding earlobes.

Step three is to make the second cut to remove a wedge-shaped amount of tissue between the "conchal bowl" and the "mastoid bone." The distance between them depends on how far out the ears protrude, but even so, it is a distance of some few millimeters. If the patient is an adult, the cartilage in the ear will likely be quite "springy" as I explained, so some cartilage might have to be removed along with the soft tissue.

Step four is to correct — or re-create — the anti-helical fold. Any seamstress or tailor will appreciate the interim step of "basting" with marking sutures exactly where the final stitches are to go. (Some surgeons use India ink or tattooing techniques, much like some seamstresses use tailor's chalk or tracing paper.) This is done to achieve as much similarity as possible between the two ears; ultimately, it's a matter of visual judgment and adjusting the basting, which again, is a lot like tailoring. An extra stitch will be used to bring the lobule in line with the plane of the newly formed anti-helical fold.

Step five is to apply the permanent sutures. They resemble a kind of "blanket" stitch and are designed not to be removed. The

Incision for flyaway ear surgery

middle suture is placed first, followed by the lower, then the upper suture. This allows for the fold to be "eased" into its proper shape. As the sutures are placed, the marking sutures, or basting stitches, are removed. This step involves only the cartilage and its membranous layer of perichondrium. Stitching of the skin will follow later.

Step six is the delicate procedure of tightening the sutures, one by one. Experience and the proper touch will produce a natural-looking anti-helical fold, with a lobule on the same plane. Unfortunately, there is a tendency on the part of less experienced surgeons to over-correct the anti-helical fold by tying the sutures too tight. This makes the fold too prominent and brings the helical rim of the ear unnaturally close to the skull.

Step seven is to reduce the protuberance of the ear, to rein in the flyaway, by threading a suture from the exposed cartilage behind the conchal bowl through the mastoid bone in the skull behind the ear.

This effectively anchors the conchal bowl into its new position, and pulls the two incisions of the flap together.

Step eight is to cut away, or excise, any excessive skin that is produced during the previous step. Once the excessive skin has been removed, the remaining edges of skin can be sutured together. These sutures are removed sometime during the second week after the operation.

Step nine is to apply a light "pressure" dressing called Kling under a three-inch-wide tensor bandage. This dressing is worn until the first postoperative visit to collect any of the normal seepage the wound might discharge. The Kling and tensor are then replaced by a much lighter dressing or sporty headband that must be worn continuously — night and day — for the next two weeks.

After two weeks, no further dressing is required, but the patient should wear an ordinary, terry-cloth sports headband at night, to prevent sleeping on either ear the wrong way. There will be some swelling for two or three weeks, but it is mostly behind the ear and hardly noticeable. The swelling will cause some discomfort, though few patients need a strong painkiller. Children and those who are particularly sensitive to pain might require Tylenol.

In rare situations, a patient could develop a reaction to the permanent sutures placed in the cartilage. The sutures actually begin to be rejected through the skin (we call this the "spitting" of sutures), and the patient suffers a recurrent sore behind or in front of the ear. The sutures can be removed quite safely nine months after surgery without jeopardizing the results because by then the scarring behind the ear has matured and become strong enough to hold the cartilage in place. If the sutures must be removed before nine months, the ear might "spring" back into its preoperative position. In this case, the otoplasty would have to be repeated. A different brand of suture, or a different method of suturing, would have to be employed.

In the twenty years that I have been practicing, I've performed several hundred otoplasties; less than five percent have had to be revised due to a patient's rejection of sutures.

Hair Transplants

THE VARIOUS NEEDS FOR FACIAL plastic surgery I've discussed so far in this book are shared equally by women and men, but much to their chagrin, there is one situation that applies almost exclusively to men. Male pattern baldness, as it is called, affects about two-thirds of men, to varying degrees. Not all of them are bothered by it, but some men suffer terribly from a loss of self-esteem or the belief that baldness makes them appear prematurely aged. Happily, there has been steady progress over the past ten years in the procedures we have to treat male pattern baldness. (There are other reasons for baldness, like disease or accident, or even stress, but I will concentrate in this chapter on male pattern baldness as the most common problem.)

Research hasn't yet revealed exactly why men go bald, though we know now that it's a genetic tendency that often comes to males from the mother's side of the family. Even though baldness can come from the father's side, if a mother's father or grandfather has shown balding, chances are good that her son will, too. Classic male pattern baldness will start to show up in some men in their early twenties, though most are afflicted in their late twenties.

Types of Male Pattern Baldness

There are three stages to the development of male pattern baldness, each more pronounced than the last. The first stage is known as "frontal temporal recession," when the hairline recedes from the temples at either side of the forehead. This stage actually appears in all men as a natural part of the aging process. However, if it becomes apparent in a young man in his twenties, chances are good that he'll continue on to the next two stages.

Stage two of male pattern baldness is when "frontal temporal recession" is combined with thinning hair on the crown or "vertex" of the head (its highest point). If a man enters stage two in his thirties, it is highly probable that he'll go on to the third stage. But if he develops this pattern of baldness later in life, say in his fifties, it's unlikely that it will become any more noticeable. These men might not progress beyond crown baldness.

Three stages of male pattern baldness

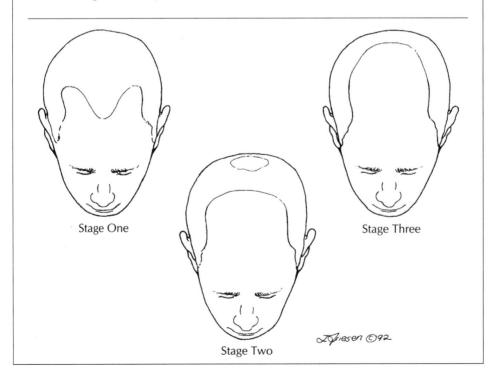

Stage One

Stage Two

Stage Three

The third stage of male pattern baldness occurs when the "frontal temporal recession" has advanced to the point that it joins with what has become a completely bald crown. The pattern is complete in stage three, and the man is left with a fringe of hair around the sides and back of his head. Some religious orders of monks, or friars, adopted the fringe as a standard of grooming in days gone by, though it's interesting to speculate what came first: the style, or the prevalence of male pattern baldness in certain influential monasteries.

Today, there are a number of different approaches to minimizing the problem of male pattern baldness through plastic surgery. But before I explain what they are, let me caution that not all balding men are good candidates for surgery.

As with every other procedure in plastic surgery, it is important that the patient understand its limitations. The surgery for baldness is not designed to restore a man's youth — he'll never have the hairline he had as a young man in his late teens or early twenties. In fact, to give him such a low, full hairline would be a disservice; it would look phony, as though he were wearing a badly fitted hairpiece. The idea is to camouflage a man's baldness, to create a hairline that is natural-looking (maybe even slightly thin and receded) in harmony with his naturally aging face. Once again, a patient with unrealistic expectations is not a good candidate for plastic surgery.

Neither is the man with very fine blond hair a good candidate. This is unfortunate, in my opinion, because I don't like to see any willing patient of plastic surgery turned down because he is the wrong "type" for it. But fine blond hair presents two problems nearly impossible to overcome. First, there is a certain amount of scarring involved with procedures to correct baldness, and fine hair will not conceal scars to the scalp. Second, fine hair means that, technically, there are not many hair follicles per square inch on the scalp, and this presents a problem — particularly if the surgical approach is a hair transplant. The "donor site" on the patient's head, as it is called, might not yield enough hair for adequate camouflage. However, patients with coarse blond hair are excellent candidates for surgery.

Timing can also affect the suitability of a candidate: if a patient seeks out plastic surgery too early in his evolution toward male pattern baldness, it might backfire later. This would be the case if a surgeon were to harvest hair for transplant from a "donor site" on the scalp that was destined to become bald later in life. The result, a few years after surgery, would be scars where the hairs had been harvested, and scars on the scalp where it had been transplanted — but no hair. In *The Face Book*, published by the American Academy of Facial Plastic and Reconstructive Surgery, a surgeon from California recounts his experience: "I've seen patients who wanted me to repair damage done by early, poorly done transplant procedures. Some have had all their donor hair used up and are left with visible scars or abnormal patterns of baldness. These men are almost tearful when I tell them nothing can be done. They would take their natural baldness back in an instant, but it is already too late."

Surgery

The surgical procedures for dealing with male pattern baldness fall into four basic categories: punch grafting; the short flap; the long "Juri" flap; and scalp reduction.

To make the proper assessment of a patient's balding pattern depends, to an extent, on when the patient makes his first appointment for treatment. If the patient shows signs of male pattern baldness in his early twenties, the surgeon will be able to warn him against too-early treatment, as I mentioned above. If, on the other hand, the patient arrives for treatment at just the right time (perhaps in his mid-thirties), the surgeon can begin to perform punch grafting about one inch behind the patient's existing hairline. This action "anticipates" the receding hairline and should make it look quite natural over the years as the original hair thins next to the transplanted hair.

Punch Grafting

Punch grafting has been around for more than thirty years, and it is sometimes used in combination with one of the other three more

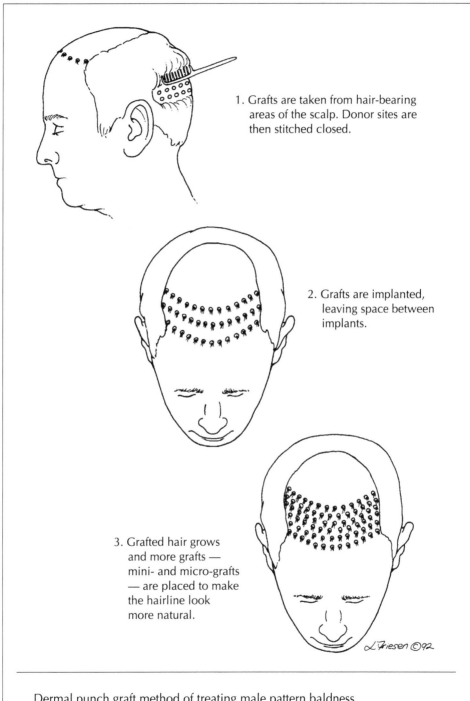

1. Grafts are taken from hair-bearing areas of the scalp. Donor sites are then stitched closed.

2. Grafts are implanted, leaving space between implants.

3. Grafted hair grows and more grafts — mini- and micro-grafts — are placed to make the hairline look more natural.

Dermal punch graft method of treating male pattern baldness.

recently developed methods. Like a lot of facial plastic surgeons, I don't do much punch grafting; it's an art that has been perfected largely by dermatologists, some of whom specialize in the procedure. Punch grafting is a technique requiring the use of tiny cylindrical "punches," each with a razor-sharp edge, that can be bored into the skin to extract a tiny transplant between three and five millimeters in diameter. (The graft resembles a core drilling sample.) The punch can be manipulated between a surgeon's thumb and forefinger if only a few grafts are needed, or it can be connected to a drill-like gun with a trigger for the removal of dozens of grafts in a single session. Each minuscule graft of skin contains hair follicles that are transplanted from one part of the patient's scalp to another, balding part of the scalp. During this procedure, the patient is in a state of "conscious sedation" under a local anesthetic.

The "donor sites" for punch grafts are usually found above a patient's ears and at the back of his head. A good donor site will have at least twelve hair shafts, or follicles, per four millimeters' diameter. At first, when punch grafting became popular, surgeons would simply plant rows of five-millimeter grafts up near the front of a patient's temples and crown to restore a forehead hairline. This procedure, revolutionary though it was, often resulted in a kind of "corn row" look: you could see the stalks of new hair plain as day against the balding pate.

To overcome this problem, surgeons began to intersperse the larger grafts with smaller, two-millimeter grafts. (No matter the size of the grafts, it is a time-consuming procedure; sometimes a dermatologist, or surgeon, will implant 100 grafts in a single session lasting up to two hours.) The interspersion helped to give a more natural look, but the technique has been refined even further within the past four or five years with the so-called mini- or micro-grafts. Now surgeons will take a single strip of hair and divide it up into sections as fine as a single hair. This is called the "square plug" method because the individual segments are square-shaped. These micro-grafts are so fine, the surgeon has only to make slitlike incisions in the scalp to insert them. The incisions bleed slightly, and the clotting factor in the blood acts to secure the grafts in place.

The surgeon who specializes in punch grafting tries to mix five- and four-millimeter grafts with square plugs to imitate the gradation of a natural hairline. Look carefully at your own hairline and you'll see that the hair at the very edge is fine like a baby's and that it gets progressively coarser further back into the scalp. Also, the hairline is not perfectly even. A surgeon who has managed to mirror these conditions has achieved high art. It requires enormous patience and painstaking attention to detail, as the sessions to complete the grafting might extend over more than five years, especially if the baldness has not been complete prior to the start of any transplant procedures.

After each session, the hair follicles from each graft fall out, then regrow to their normal adult size and shape. Patients can wash their hair — gently — during the first week after grafting, but it is important not to disturb the plugs. The scalp will look slightly "cobble-stoned" until the hair regrows to cover it.

Flaps

The patient who shows up for the first time in a surgeon's office in an advanced, stage-three condition of male pattern baldness presents a challenge. This is the sort of patient who is quite often referred on to a facial cosmetic surgeon, for treatment with the more intensive techniques of short and long flap surgery, and scalp reduction. (I am not saying that stage-three patients are the only ones who benefit from these techniques — in fact, I prefer to treat all balding patients with a combination of the four basic methods.) Again, it is wise to remember that facial plastic surgery has its limitations; the classic "billiard ball" dome can be improved upon, but not entirely restored to its former, hirsute glory.

Short flap surgery is ideal for the older patient who is unlikely to progress beyond stage one of male pattern baldness; he is about fifty and has some "frontal temporal recession." A flap is like a graft, but different from other grafts in that it remains attached to the scalp at one end even while it is rotated into a new position. The scalp is the skin and associated subcutaneous tissues that cover the upper part of

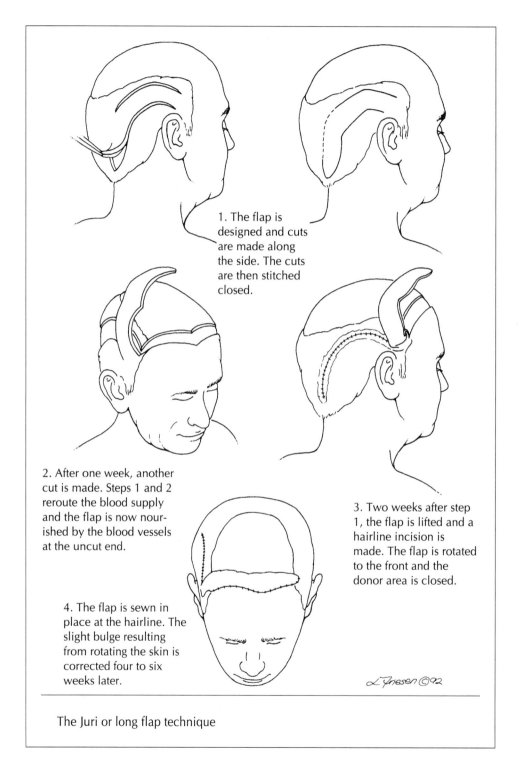

1. The flap is designed and cuts are made along the side. The cuts are then stitched closed.

2. After one week, another cut is made. Steps 1 and 2 reroute the blood supply and the flap is now nourished by the blood vessels at the uncut end.

3. Two weeks after step 1, the flap is lifted and a hairline incision is made. The flap is rotated to the front and the donor area is closed.

4. The flap is sewn in place at the hairline. The slight bulge resulting from rotating the skin is corrected four to six weeks later.

The Juri or long flap technique

the head. To create the short flaps, a section of bald skin in each of the temples is excised, or cut out, while the patient is under local anesthetic. Correspondingly sized sections of skin from behind the hairline — complete with hair follicles — are raised with one end still attached to the scalp, and rotated to settle into the excised area. The wounds left behind by the transferred flaps are pulled together and stitched closed; scars are hidden by the patient's own hair.

The flaps must be cut on a slight diagonal angle at the point of incision. Similarly, the skin surrounding the transplanted flaps must be cut on an angle, so that the two meet at a beveled edge. This allows the hair follicles in the transplanted flaps to grow up and through the natural scar tissue that will form as a result of surgery.

The technical details a surgeon must consider with short flap surgery include the possibility that there might be a certain "fullness," or bunching up of skin, where the flaps were rotated. (Try rotating sections of a heavier material like corduroy and you'll see what I mean.) Sometimes, this bunching up or kinking, which we call a "dog ear," settles down by itself within six weeks, but often it doesn't and minor surgical revision is necessary to reduce the kinking, again under a local anesthetic.

Long "Juri" flap surgery, so-named for the first surgeon to perfect the technique, is ideal for patients who are headed toward stage two or three of male pattern baldness. (The Juri flap has since been modified by two surgeons: now, some doctors refer to the Fleming-Mayer flap, which is slightly different in length and width.) Like short flap surgery, it involves lifting a flap of skin with hair follicles from the skull and rotating to the new hairline. However, the flap is much longer in this case, extending from the side to the very back of the head. (If two such flaps are necessary to complete the procedure, the flaps would be correspondingly sized on either side and meet at the mid-line of the back of the head.) The long flap is then draped over the crown of the head to restore hair to the balding vertex. If two flaps are used, they are placed one in front of the other, to cover a wider area. Each flap is about four centimeters wide.

Because the Juri flap is so long — up to twenty-eight centimeters — the entire procedure must be completed in steps over a period of time, what the medical profession calls delayed surgery. By extending the surgery over two weeks, we are training the blood supply to go along the same axis as the flap (or along the length of the flap). Also, the flap becomes accustomed to a lowered supply of oxygen while the blood redirects its flow (blood is the bearer of oxygen throughout the body). This will help the flap to survive the healing process once it has been transplanted. Without the precaution of delayed surgery, the end of the flap would likely die.

The first step is to mark out the flap and cut seventy-five percent of its perimeter while the patient is under local anesthetic. Dressings applied to the wound can be removed the following day. One week later, again while the patient is under local anesthetic, the "end" of the flap, that part closest to the back of the head, is lifted up and down to disrupt any healing, then restored to its position under a dressing that can be removed the next day. Another week passes before the patient returns to have the flap lifted and rotated into its new position, completing the surgery. As with the short flap, the "dog ears" will have to be corrected six weeks after the operation if they don't settle down of their own accord.

The wound left where the Juri flap was harvested is pulled together and closed up with sutures. However, because the longer flap is so much wider, this part of the procedure really amounts to a neck-lift. The scalp and loose neck tissue are pulled up and closed just as they would be for the more extensive operation of a face-lift. The chapter on face-lifts (Chapter Six) provides more details.

After flap surgery, it is wise to avoid washing the scalp or combing the hair for a couple of days, and then only gently. A patient in the habit of having his head massaged should not resume the practice for a couple of weeks. I advise against a too-vigorous massage even after the flap surgery is completely healed.

Both short flap and long flap surgery for male pattern baldness provide the instant result of a new hairline. Some men are delighted by this, others with incomplete male pattern baldness prefer the less dramatic change of punch grafting. However, as I mentioned earlier,

I often use a combination of techniques to create the most natural-looking hairline. In addition to flaps and punch grafting, I also perform scalp reduction surgery, if it is warranted.

Scalp Reduction

Scalp reduction surgery literally reduces the area of bald scalp on a patient's head. In most cases, the scalp is malleable enough that hair-bearing skin can be stretched and brought together; the bald skin in between is cut out. This is ideally done before other procedures like flap surgery or punch grafting as it reduces the amount of area that has to be treated for baldness. Scalp skin is much thicker and tougher than you might imagine, and it has few nerve endings, so there is not much pain associated with scalp reduction, though some patients experience a kind of tingling sensation for up to six months after the surgery.

Scalp Expansion

Sometimes the patient's scalp is too tight for the conventional approach to scalp reduction. In this case, we have to stretch the skin first before pulling it together. *The Face Book* has a succinct account of the procedure: "In this procedure, the surgeon implants a deflated balloon under the skin of the hair-bearing scalp. Twice a week, sterile water [known as 'normal saline' — a saltwater solution] is injected into the balloon, stretching the skin slightly. A pulling feeling may be noted for a day or so, but then the skin relaxes. Injections continue over a period of six to eight weeks, until the desired expansion has been achieved. Then the balloon is removed, the bald area cut away, and the newly stretched hair-bearing scalp used to cover the area."

With this technique, more crown scalp can be removed, which means that less hair is needed to cover the bald area. Quite rightly, *The Face Book* passage ends with the advice: "If you require tissue expansion, take along a large hat and a sense of humor." Patients are a frightful sight with two bags growing out of their head during the later stages of the procedure, but the means to the end are worthwhile.

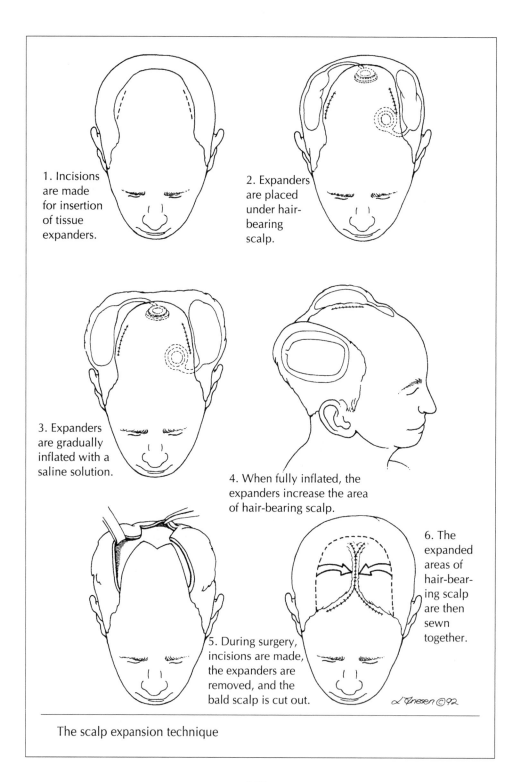

1. Incisions are made for insertion of tissue expanders.

2. Expanders are placed under hair-bearing scalp.

3. Expanders are gradually inflated with a saline solution.

4. When fully inflated, the expanders increase the area of hair-bearing scalp.

5. During surgery, incisions are made, the expanders are removed, and the bald scalp is cut out.

6. The expanded areas of hair-bearing scalp are then sewn together.

The scalp expansion technique

Each of the surgical procedures for treating male pattern baldness has attendant complications. There is always the slim possibility that punch grafts will fail to "take," or that hair follicles within the grafts won't grow. (This is especially true with the new micro-grafts of a single hair follicle; the root of the follicle is more easily damaged in such a small graft.) And, as I described, the very end of a long flap might die, despite precautionary delayed surgery. (This is especially true with patients who are smokers because smoking affects the micro-circulation of the scalp skin.) However, if it does, a surgeon can do repair work to retain the new hairline with some punch grafts and smaller flaps.

All such surgery might cause a patient to bruise and swell around the eyes and behind the ears, though the swelling will subside in about two weeks. During this time, the patient should avoid any activity that would place a strain on the affected area, especially if it has been punch grafted. (The grafts can pop out with vigorous combing, for example.) After flap surgery, a turban-style bandage must be worn for a couple of days, and if any stitches have been used, they will be removed about a week after the operation. Within six weeks, most patients should be able to resume all normal activity.

There is very little pain associated with plastic surgery for male pattern baldness, just the tingling or tight sensation I mentioned earlier.

In Closing...

I SINCERELY HOPE that those of you who have taken the time to read this book are now fully confident about what to expect from a facial cosmetic surgeon. Facial cosmetic surgery is not the work of magicians, as I have explained, but rather the ability of well trained specialists to find beauty where it exists and show it to a patient's best advantage.

Finding beauty is sometimes a humble matter of disguising a scar or removing the bump from a nose. Other times, it does have magical qualities if we are able to restore a patient's dignity with reconstructive surgery following an accident, or restore a patient's confidence by altering the more obvious effects of aging. But most of the time, finding beauty in all its variety comes from within — when a patient connects with the self-esteem that shines through every gesture, and every expression, to make the world a better place.

I leave you now with a few words by Carl Gustav Jung, in his book *Modern Man in Search of a Soul:*

> "Aging people should know that their lives are not
> mounting and unfolding, but that an inexorable inner pro-
> cess forces the contraction of life.

For a young person it is almost a sin — and certainly a danger — to be too much occupied with himself but for the aging person it is a duty and a necessity to give serious attention to himself."

And finally, a word of thanks to my patients for their goodwill, trust and encouragement. Without them, this book would not have been possible.

For general information concerning facial cosmetic surgery or surgeons, contact the **Canadian Academy of Facial Plastic and Reconstructive Surgery**, Suite 401, Mount Sinai Hospital, 600 University Avenue, Toronto, Ontario M5G 1X5 (416) 569-6965; **The American Academy of Facial Plastic Reconstructive Surgery** at 1-800-523-3223

or the following provincial bodies:

College of Physicians and Surgeons of Alberta
9901-108 Street, Edmonton, Alberta   T5K 1G9
(403) 423-4764

College of Physicians and Surgeons of British Columbia
1807 W. 10th Avenue, Vancouver, B.C. V6J 2A9
(604) 733-7758

College of Physicians and Surgeons of Manitoba
494 St. James Street, Winnipeg, Manitoba R3G 3J4
(204) 774-4344

College of Physicians and Surgeons of New Brunswick
Suite 1078, 400 Main Street, Saint John, New Brunswick E2K 4N5
(506) 658-0959

Newfoundland Medical Board
15 Rowan Street, St. John's, Newfoundland A1B 2X2
(709) 726-8546

Provincial Medical Board of Nova Scotia
Suite 3050, 1515 South Park Street, Halifax, Nova Scotia B3J 2L2
(902) 422-5823

College of Physicians and Surgeons of Ontario
80 College Street, Toronto, Ontario M5G 2E2
(416) 961-1711

College of Physicians and Surgeons of Prince Edward Island
199 Grasston Street, Charlottetown, P.E.I. C1A 1L2
(902) 566-3861

College of Physicians and Surgeons of Quebec
Suite 914, 1440 Ste.-Catherine West, Montreal, Quebec H3G 1S5
(514) 878-4441

College of Physicians and Surgeons of Saskatchewan
211 Fourth Avenue South, Saskatoon, Saskatchewan S7K 1N1
(306) 244-7355

A P P E N D I X I I

Estimated Price List for the more common facial cosmetic procedures - in Canadian dollars (1992)

		Minimum	Maximum
Collagen injections		1cc for $350	1 cc for $400
Chemical Peel:	Total face	$1,500	$4,000
	Lower eyelids	500	1,000
	Lips & chin	500	1,000
Superficial Peels		200	600
Upper & Lower Blepharoplasty		3,500	4,500
Upper Blepharoplasty		2,000	2,500
Lower Blepharoplasty		2,600	3,000
Oriental Double Eyelidplasty		2,000	3,500
Forehead Lift		3,000	4,500
Facelift/Liposuction		4,500	6,000
Malar Implants (cheek implants)		3,500	4,500
Implants to lip cheek grooves		2,000	3,000
Implants to marionette grooves		1,500	2,500
Total Rhinoplasty		3,500	4,500
Partial Rhinoplasty		2,500	3,500
Otoplasty		3,000	4,000
Lip reductions		2,500	3,000
Lip augmentations		2,500	3,000
Lower face/neck liposuction		2,500	3,500
Mentoplasty		3,000	4,000

Combination procedures:

Fee reductions occur when multiple procedures are performed at the same time.

Provincial Health Insurance coverage:
Most provincial health insurance plans in Canada cover the following:

• facial scar revision
• dermabrasion for acne scarring
• otoplasty if the patient is under 18 years of age
• traumatic crooked noses with trauma occurring within two years

Revisional cosmetic procedures:
Revisional cosmetic procedures must be charged to the patient; they are not covered by provincial health care plans. If the surgeon performed the original surgery, the price for revisional work may be 50% of the original fee, depending on the complexity of the work or it may be included in the original fee. Ask your surgeon prior to the original surgery.

If the previous surgery was performed by another surgeon, the fee may be at least 50% more, depending on the complexity.

APPENDIX III

Further Reading

The Face Book

The Teen Face Book

both can be obtained from
the American Academy of Facial Plastic and Reconstructive Surgery
Suite 220, 1110 Vermont Avenue
Washington, DC 20005-3522 USA

Telephone: (202) 842-4500

or Fax: (202) 371-1514

DAVID A.F. ELLIS, MD, FRCS(C), FACS graduated from the University of Toronto Medical School in 1966. Dr. Ellis completed his fellowship residency training in Otolaryngology at the University of Toronto. Immediately following this residency, Dr. Ellis took a post-residency fellowship in Facial Plastic and Reconstructive Surgery.

Dr. Ellis opened his practice in Toronto in 1973; it consisted of private practice as well as teaching Otolaryngology and Facial Plastic Surgery at the University of Toronto. He did his teaching through appointments at the Toronto Hospital and through an appointment at the Toronto Western Hospital. Dr. Ellis is also on staff at Etobicoke General Hospital.

Dr. Ellis was chairman of Continuing Medical Education of his university department from 1984 to 1988. He has been Director of CME programs at the University of Toronto; since 1984 he has been a moderator of Telemedicine (Distant Education) for the Department of Otolaryngology; he has been invited to lecture on Facial Plastic Surgery for numerous continuing medical education programs run by the American Academy of Facial Plastic and Reconstructive Surgery and many American and Canadian universities. He has also written many papers for medical publications.

Dr. Ellis is past president of the Canadian Institute of Facial Plastic Surgery, past Canadian vice-president of the American Academy of Facial Plastic and Reconstructive Surgery and the Past Secretary of the Canadian Society of Otolaryngology - Head and Neck Surgery.

KAREN O'REILLY has been a freelance writer since the 1980s. Her work has appeared in *The Globe and Mail*, several Canadian magazines and on CBC-television. In 1990, she co-wrote *Running Risks* with Martin O'Malley and Angella Issajenko.

Index